Understanding the Purpose of Time

Maximizing Your Life of Fulfillment

Neba Akongnwi Fuh

Copyright©2023

Neba Akongnwi Fuh
Contact: 676787999
akongnwismart@gmail.com

ISBN: 978-9956-549-17-7

Edited by PATAMAE Research and Editing Consultancy
paddyama@yahoo.com   (237)675959969

Understanding the Purpose of Time – Motivational 1title 2023

Dedication

For all who fail to manage time well

Contents

Acknowledgements

Special gratitude to my heavenly Father for the unexpected writing grace bestowed on me; to my parents and family members who took the time to read, correct or encourage me; my caring mother particularly was always there for me; my uncle Dr Ndongmanji John Niba painstakingly did several readings of the work, a feat reserved only for a loving uncle. Friends' encouragement gave me personal value and the push to forge on.

Miss Angu Pride, with Mr Angu Vigilant Ade and their editorial team, were a honing company for this work. Miss Shu Barbara equally did me no small favour by accepting my offer to proofread. Your contributions were invaluable. Finally, PATAMAE Research and Editing Consultancy's CEO critiqued and then gave his professional clearance for the work to go to the press.

I remain eternally grateful for all your input and efforts. It is a work with push and help from many ends but I take the blame for any misuse of the assistance you all gave me.

The Common Denominator

Whatever you invest your time in, you become. Your life is how you use your time.
- Myles Munroe

Bestselling author and motivational speaker Brian Tracy in his book; 'Time Power' says that the question of purpose – the reason for our existence, is the question that is most asked by everyone on the planet. The ultimate goal of every man, and woman, is to live life to the fullest marked by life fulfilment, high productivity, the accomplishment of a worthy goal or ideal, and a tremendous feeling of happiness. In effect, we are all in search of ways to make our lives more meaningful, impactful, and truly successful. So we go about seeking the right relationships, lifestyle ingredients, career choices, skill sets, ideas, and other activities which when engaged in, will give us that which we desire. Our quest for happiness and success is a destination that many believe exists, but are unable to trail. Yet the way to happiness is not hidden; if a man devotes time, energy, tenacity, and passion to searching for what he wants, nature being just and fair will lead him to it.

The signal issue is time, which to human activities is like soil to the seed, the means to get dreams, ideas, plans, and talents from their dwelling places within individuals into the world. Time is the means both to serve others and to bring us profit. All our goals can be realized by constructive time usage – doing every day, however small it may be, the things that will lead to the accomplishment of said goals. Time has a powerful way of making things fall into place. All that is required is for us to use every second of it conscientiously, doing what ought to be done, as every second, minute, or hour of the day ticking away does not return and cannot be retrieved.

History bears witness to the importance and relevance of time in the purpose fulfilment equation. Most success stories will attest to the fact that without the proper management of time, and its allocation to worthwhile ideals, they probably would have died in obscurity. Success is really about spending time in fruitful ventures. How you spend your time, and what you spend it on matters. It is a principle vindicated in the life stories of all great achievers, biblical figures no exception.

We all have been gifted with diverse gifts and ideas that can effect meaningful changes in our generations, yet, their realization is primarily hinged on how we spend our time. Everything about our lives and results can change if we would but spend time differently. Everyone yearns to be the best possible, even when that best is blurred by imprecision. Nobody wants to end up broke, frustrated, at the bottom, regretting why they didn't do the things they knew they were called to do, or able to do. We all want to make our lives meaningful and fulfilling and we surely can. The how is answered by Wilfred Peterson: *by focusing our inherent powers as well as our time, energy, finances, and other resources in doing the things we always have had a burning desire to accomplish.*

The life of every tree lies in its seed and until that seed is planted and allowed to grow over time, the joy of harvest and purpose fully deployed will forever be deprived from that tree. Your joy, in like manner, is within your purpose and potential, and idea. It will only be made manifest when you take out quality time to plant it, time to cater to it, and time to watch it grow.

This book looks at the various ways in which to maximize time and avoid waste. It focuses on time management, the way to save more time and direct it to well-conceived ends. It projects this management as an urgency to be tackled immediately and always by speed and purposive activities. Perhaps the start off point is the fact that you have a lot to offer in life.

However, you will never amount to much if you don't resolve to be ruthless and highly disciplined with how you manage and spend your time. With a poignant sense of urgency, you can maximize the time you have.

As you go through this book it is hoped that you will be raised to greater awareness of what it takes to maximize time which logically translates to effectiveness and life fulfilment. This then is an introduction to the various principles needed for a complete change in your life.

Part One

The Purpose of Time

God gives us everything for a reason. Until that reason is found out, we are likely to misuse the gift. Like the sun that was created to act as the greater light for the day and the moon for the night, time too has a great purpose. Our lives and gifts are bound to be wasted unless that purpose blooms.

Chapter 1

The Concept of Time

Everything that happens in this world happens at a time God chooses... He has set the right time for everything.

\-   Ecclesiastes3:1, 11 _GNT

One thing we have all been given equal amounts of is time – a most precious resource from God via which our goals, ideas, and purpose, can be birthed and groomed. Consequently, the way you use your time today will be reflected in the results you will obtain sometime in the future. You become whatever you repeatedly invest time in.

Like all other principles governed by nature, time strictly obeys the law of cause and effect. This law states that nature is neutral and that everything happens for a reason; a cause has to be initiated for every effect desired.

Circumstances unfold, not by chance, but as consequences or effects proceeding from specific causes we initiate. All the things we would desire to have, all achievements we would love to realize, and all goals we would love to attain can be classified as effects that will only proceed from specific causes or actions we must implement. Results do not come by chance but by the initiation of clearly conceived actions (*causes*) which in turn produce the desired outcomes (*effects*). The implication is clear; doing things that are of no value to your life, things not related to your life goals or the progress of your dreams, aspirations, and ideas, cannot be expected to bring about success.

Time, like life, obeys the law of cause and effect always. Hence, for valuable life results, we must invest it in productive aims and value-adding pursuits. Identify, activate, develop, and build on as well as deploy your most precious and inherent gifts and potentials. Put your time to value by doing what you know will enable you to realize your dreams, give birth to your ideas and fulfil the divine assignment for your life. That is the sure way to leave a mark on the earth.

The Value of Time

It has to be stated ad nauseam in the process of this book that time is the most precious and priceless of God-given resources. It endows us with the capacity to transform and bring to reality the dreams and ideas which God has laid in our hearts to fulfil. It is more important, more flexible, and more diversely applicable than money. It is so vital that without its efficient use, our purpose and entire destinies are lost. On the other hand, proper time management and efficient time utilization will result in proper life management, accomplishment, and fulfilment.

Every goal we would ever want to accomplish in life has its accomplishment wrapped around how we spend our time and what we spend this time doing. No matter how much we desire and aspire, it is how effectively and efficiently we use the resources at our disposal that lead us to our goal; good intentions will never be a substitute for prompt and decisive action.

It is not enough to want to be successful or to envisage the pleasurable rewards that come with success. You are not going to make money simply because you know how convenient it will be to never have financial problems again. No. Goals are not reached simply by luck, but by clearly conceived and goal-oriented actions, which yield the expected outcomes when continually and diligently engaged in. The ambience and facilitating ingredient in all activity is time, and it needs to be most judiciously managed.

Time is the principal factor and like a seed cannot grow until it finds favourable soil, the hopes of realizing the object of our dreams, no matter how plausible they may be, fall short until they get planted in suitable farms of time. Indeed, you become whatever you invest your time in and your life is how you use your time. This is what Brian Tracy rhythmically expresses: "Manage your time, manage your life." Conversely, mismanage your time, and mismanage your life. And while time is indestructible since we cannot waste it, when we mismanage time, we are wasting our lives, and frustrating the possibilities of realizing our dreams.

You become whatever you invest your time in. Your life is how you use your time

---

There is then, to repeat Ecclesiastes, a time for everything – a time to sow and a time to reap. Ultimately, we all have a timeframe within which to plant the seeds we want, bearing in mind that tomorrow we will harvest from our time farms the fruits of what we plant today, good or bad. For every useful or useless information or activity you sow, a definite fruit is awaited. Understanding this fact about our lives in connection to how we spend our time is therefore expedient and highly valuable for those who would fully realize their dreams and accomplish all they would. And we do not need to look too far into the horizons of time for the future is one second away from the now.

It stands to reason that we should make the most of our time ensuring that we plant good, useful, valuable, and highly productive seeds in it today.

The CPU of Life

As the Central Processing Unit (C.P.U) is to computers in the computing world, so also is time to man – the processing unit of our lives. By it, we input events to be processed for a corresponding output. Like all processing units, time follows the *Garbage In, Garbage Out* (GIGO) principle. Your future outputs will be a function of your present inputs; you will receive at a later time just what you invest in the present, perhaps amplified and embellished.

Beyond momentary satisfaction, spending time today on unproductive schemes and events ends up adding no value to your life. Desultory living, even in the perception of the least conscientious person, is not expected to yield productive results. Success, happiness, and a sense of fulfilment tomorrow require focal use of today. Know the things that lead to your great expectations and then spend time today doing them. If you aspire to be a great leader tomorrow, therefore, you need to spend quality time today studying, and acquiring the skills and aptitudes necessary for excellence. To pass your end-of-course exams, spend more time on your books, preparing for them. To make it in life, you must be willing to sacrifice unprofitable and time-wasting frivolities for profitable but perhaps unpleasant activities that you know will lead to success.

Life is a business transaction with time as the currency. You pay for a great tomorrow with a great deal of time today spent on pursuits that will add value to your life — pursuits, and activities that take you steps closer to attaining your life goals.

The truth underlying this business deal of life is that the way to the top is not normally by chance. The great men and women who make a difference in our world today give up short-term gratification, putting in the extra effort and efficiently using their time to create value. It becomes a virtual slogan that true success is a long-term investment. Sitting around and being awed by the heights is no way of rising to the heights. Exaggerated time for relaxing, watching TV, idling on social media, and having fun is not the way to high places. In snippets and catchphrases, the principle is rhythmically and regularly expressed:

High achievers are usually proficient resource managers; efficiently managing their resources – time inclusive. This puts them in a better position to maximize opportunities and when said opportunities arise, they move up the ladder, often at rapid rates. Thus by a conscious decision to identify, accept, build, refine, and polish their skills the great grow. They do not leave their lives to chance merely or to an overnight lucky catch. No. Greatness takes time readying the skills that get rewarded later, sometimes at least expected, and rather magical moments. This is not a truth to overlook and expect by sudden flight to land at the top. Any such semblance of growth is speedily reversed. As the saying goes: quick come, quick go. The higher the structure is to rise, the deeper the foundation should be. Shortcuts are hazards of unsure outcomes.

Garbage In Garbage Out

If you put in enough sleep today, you will inevitably be friends with poverty tomorrow. If you are lazy and idle today, you will wallow in frustration, lack, and want tomorrow. If you are not serious about your studies today, be ready to live a life of mediocrity and painful struggle tomorrow. If you spend too much time on fleeting pleasures and instant gratification today – watching movies, playing video games, partying, and clubbing – be ready to reap an average, underproductive, and sweat-full life tomorrow. The logic is GIGO: the junk you put in at this end (today) comes out at the other end (tomorrow).

If, on the other hand, you devote quality time to value-adding pursuits today, consciously implementing measures to realize a predetermined life goal or idea, your efforts will no doubt pay off tomorrow. If you spend time working at becoming better at your craft, or God-given abilities, the future will eventually bring you better rewards. No matter how complicated it is to calculate it, the bottom line is that life is fair, giving each their due rather than what they feel entitled to.

Your tomorrow is closely knit to your today as your success or failure is hinged to, nay, it is the other side of what you spend today on. If you have the hindsight to look keenly at your yesterday, you will find that you are in this state and status today due to what you worked out practically yesterday. Your current disposition is a function of your decisions and actions in the past. Luck and the other unforeseen are the nuances of our own choices, shaded but not completely blocked from our vision. Today's outputs for you are flowing from your inputs of yesterday; they are a function of your investment of quality time in the past.

It could not be louder said that nature never discriminates; it is no respecter of persons and does not simply give people what they wish, but what they deserve. Failure or success in life is primarily a personal choice, not the doing of the environment, family, or boss. This does not argue against the influences impacted on our starting point by circumstances and other people, but it is what we make of what we have that decides what we get or turn out to be. We only reap what we sow.

Time then is the processing unit of life and what you get as your output is the amplified version of what you put in. This counsels us to spend our time wisely, investing it in worthwhile activities, activities whose accomplishments have a direct, positive, rewarding, and fulfilling effect on our advancements towards living a fulfilling life and in our overall progress towards attaining our core goals and life aspirations.

Without a doubt, like money, time can be stolen, abused, lost, squandered, appreciated, depreciated, and devalued. The trick is to know its importance, choose what to spend it on, who to spend it with, and where to spend it. Where you will end up in the future depends on this. Without the adequate and efficient use of your time today, you never will fulfil your life purpose or complete the assignment or mission divinely ordained for you. And misery is the inexorable result of life wasted.

Key Points

- Time is the most precious resource endowed with the capacity to transform and bring our God-given dreams and ideas to reality.
- We each have 24 hours each day to invest or waste and accept the consequences.
- Time management is life management: what you spend your time doing today is practically what your life will result in in the not-too-distant future.
- Whatever you invest your time in, you become. Your life is how you spend your time.
- Life is a business transaction and time is its currency. To be great tomorrow, spend a great deal of time today on activities that add value to your life and take you a step closer to your goal of greatness.
- What we achieve in life tomorrow is the amplification of what we put into our time machines today. It is the GIGO principle of life.

Chapter 2

The Nature of Time

Whatever you invest your time in you become. Your life is how you use your time

\-   Myles Munroe

Time is so much of the essence of life that wasting it is wasting life itself and killing or frustrating all hopes of life fulfilment. Understanding this is radically transforming. Wasting time is killing your dreams which is the practice and way to perpetual sorrow and regret.

Time for many is treated as a casual commodity, even though it is vital to success and fulfilment, the focal raison d'être of this life. Its misuse is the key to the abode of failure, struggle, and regret, which argues for the fact that it matters how you spend time.

Since there never will be enough time to do everything we would want, successful living requires engaging success tools such as prioritization and sacrifice. The not-so-important things are to be sacrificed for the really important ones. This is a way of gaining time and channelling it to more productive pursuits. As Brian Tracy states; "There is never enough time to do everything, but there is always enough time to do the most important thing.

There always will be so much to do and less time to perfectly do them. But that is no reason to fall short of goal attainment, of failing in the accomplishment of our dreams, or of fully realizing and maximizing our potential. We have no excuse. Important projects are executed by making the conscious decision to stop wasting time on distractions and other activities that add no value or benefit, and to channel this time to those that do. Although the drawbacks of procrastination will be discussed in a later chapter, it is not out of place here to state that the time to start paying more attention to important pursuits and activities is now, immediately.

There is absolutely nothing to be achieved from wasting time in distracted pursuits of everything and nothing in particular. Therefore, focusing on the valuable, profitable, and really important activities linked in some way to your destiny, vision, or life's mission is the core business of life. This calls for the redemption of time; it calls for focus, discipline, and gainful application to priorities.

Five core priorities define everyone's life, focusing on which puts every other thing in its place. Like the wheels of the car, these priorities can roll on with the entire activity structure;

1)   Spiritual Growth: Growing in our relationship with the Creator and ensuring the perennially progressive fruitfulness of our service in his vineyard;
2)   Potential Maximization: Identification, maximization, and application of personal potentials.
3)   Devotion to Career: Putting in our utmost best in duty, career, or employment.
4)   Capacity Building: Continued self-development – spirit, soul (mental, and intellectual,) and body (physical).
5) Building Relationships: Quality time with family, loved ones, and value-adding friends.

Doing all it takes to get better in every one of these areas yields astonishing results. Granted, the framing of these points does not exactly fit the sentiments of everybody, but each person has a set of similar priorities to be identified and engaged in. I call them my core life priorities. Without them, your life and time become dissipated and wasteful attempts at irrelevancies, for success relates to life goals that can only be reached by stringent prioritization.

The Limited Nature of Time

Regret is rather too common a phenomenon for many, particularly the elderly who, looking back at their lives, are often overwhelmed with distress. This distress is none other than regret for time spent on unproductive schemes. Investing time in value-adding events to fulfil their dreams would have spared them regret. Not having read in the book of nature or other realities that time is limited, they never properly invested it, but squandered it in youthful pleasures. These people frame their regret in expressions such as: "If I could go back in time with the knowledge I have now, things really will be different," or, "If I knew back then what I know now, I certainly would have made better choices and better use of my time – my life would have been different."

Of course, these are picturesque forms of the English "a stitch in time saves nine" and other familiar proverbs all enunciating the importance of judiciously utilizing time and other resources. The lesson from the regrets of others, whether for the young or old, is that time is so high a valuable commodity that it should only be put to deliberate and fruitful use. You don't have any extra time, so it will be wise to make the most of what you still have. Mistakes ignorantly committed, misplaced values, loss of focus, and lack of knowledge as to the true value of time are sad hindsight on energy, finances, potentials, and dream realizations. We can all be spared that by knowledge and practical application of time in priority ventures.

The infinite wisdom of scripture has portrayed time as something in short supply: "Teach us to number our days that we may apply our hearts to wisdom" (Psalms 90:12). This is surely another way of enjoining us to use it with care and purposeful intent. Our numbered days each have specific portions of work allocation. Over time, such work engagements become life achievements. That is how our accomplishments place us in the positions we have earned through daily input; remember that we do not rise to positions by simply desiring to. And although the psalmist warns of the shortness in supply of time, sufficient time has been given to each person to do what is of lasting value. Beyond interpreting the psalm as cautioning us to manage time well, the idea of a short supply of time can be considered a convenient myth to explain away the detriments of its misuse, i.e., shortness of time is time mismanagement, which is an untenable and lazy excuse.

In place of the lazy excuse, we should simply stop misusing, wasting, squandering, devaluing, or complaining about it and instead make the most of the time we have. Allotting too much time to battles that leave you with little or no spoils (rewards), and spending too much time on events you normally should be spending lesser time on – these are time wasters. Start allocating greater portions of time to events that build you up, bring out the best in you, and enable you to realize the future you aspire to have.

Emphatically, success is obtained through the investment of time, energy, and resources in carefully outlined steps to realize the goals or success visions aspired. If wishes were horses, we would all wish our way to the top. But success is via work not wishes merely: it is the product of time and all the other resources necessary for the realization of a goal, invested in productive predetermined pursuits.

The steps are, first, to map out a course for your life by prioritizing your focus and then to apply all said resources, passion, and enthusiasm to realize them. With ever-increasing determination and undivided attention, charge out to bring home your dreams. In the light of desultory wastefulness, time is short and limited and should be made the most of. But there is enough time for the right things and all you need is to maximize the moment. This argues for what has been termed the 80/20 Rule or the Pareto Principle.

The 80/20 Rule

The business of life is a careful selection of what matters to account for all that must be taken care of. The 80/20 rule assumes that most of the things we do in life are not vital to life. The principle, originally conceived by Italian economist, Vilfredo Pareto, states that for many outcomes, roughly 80% of consequences (results) come from 20% of causes (the "vital few"). To better explain, the theory puts the figure 80 on 100 for what might, in other words, be considered garbage or low-value activities, and 20 on 100 for the essentials. Accordingly, 80% of our actions yield only 20% of the value. There are other vital actions – supposedly only 20% of all we would normally do, that account for the remaining 80% of value.

Although Pareto's principle was originally coined to address matters of population and wealth distribution, the theory has rapidly spread through the business ecosystem, and, recently, the world of personal development, and productivity. Following this philosophy, efficient time managers do not try to do everything. They simply focus 80% of their resources, time inclusive, on the 20% of activities that give them 80% results. The 80% results are judged to be a good pass mark on human endeavours. Figures aside, on the individual level, this is a call for the redemption of time, for discipline, and for gainful application to things directly linked to our destiny, vision, or mission. It is a call to focus and careful prioritization.

The Fleeting Nature of Time

It is common to hear comments like, "I can't believe another year has gone by" or "It seems like only yesterday". Our lives fly along with the speeding time. Realizing this should make us conscious of our focus and activities. For there is no doubt that time, along with life, is fleeting and that it should be yoked to purposefulness, a concept implied by the philosopher's familiar quote that there is a time for everything – an appropriate time to plant if you are expecting to harvest. The seeds you plant also matter and predicate the harvest. And surprisingly so, they are what you choose to spend your time on. It is on the strength of your purpose alone that you can claim to be living a meaningful life.

One help in determining purposefulness is brought on by urgency. Supposing you learned that you only had one week to live, what would you spend time doing, avoiding, redoing, saying, or writing? What passions would you engage in? What talents would you maximize, skill deploy, idea realize, goal accomplish, career prospects pursue, love share before you die? If you are not doing these things now, just what are you waiting for? In these emergencies – these necessities – lie your purpose and there is no point holding them over to a vague future. It is time to take up the challenge. Every time you postpone to a later day what you should have done the day before, time passes you by. When you get distracted, time pays the price. It never waits, never stands still for you to go fool around in frivolities before coming back to proceed with the right activities. It is up to you to read the signs and redeem it.

24 hours is all the time we have per day. What have you been spending yours on? A conscious decision is required to give meaning to every passing second – to every passing second of your life. It is the little things done regularly in the ticking seconds that build up to the total of life accomplishments. Each second is an opportunity to learn something new or input something great in the cumulated but numbered days on earth

that you have. There is no spare or extra time reserved anywhere. The successes we aspire to, and should invest in, depends on this common time-lapse. It is a question of doing all we can, while we can, the best way we can in the measured timeframe we have been given. King David's prayer to understand the fragile nature of time, so he could channel every second of what time he had left to realize God's purpose for him (Ps. 90:12) should also be our prayer. For when all is said and done, time is but a gift from God for which we have to render full accounts of how we spend it.

What If...

For the past 33 years, I have looked in the mirror every morning and asked myself: 'If today were the last day of my life, would I want to do what I am about to do?' And whenever the answer has been 'No' for too many days in a row, I know I need to change something.

-   Steve Jobs

To revert to the question already posed differently, were today your last day, would you be at what you are at right now?

Key Points

1. Success is not obtained via wishes, but by the investment of time, energy, and finances in pursuits vital to the success desired.
2. Although limited how we use time is key to all we were created to do, influencing, impacting, and changing the lives we were created to impact and change.
3. There is never enough time to do everything, but there is always enough time to do the most important things.
4. Time, with life, is fragile and short; make the most of it, by being purpose driven.
5. Time waits for no one, respects no one, and does not attend to what you postpone.
6. What would you do if you had only a week left to live?
7. There is an acceptable season and there are appropriate seeds. The harvest of the future will depend on the season and the seeds you plant.

Part Two

Time Wasters

All things are lawful unto me, but all things are not expedient: all things are lawful for me, but I will not be brought under the power of any.

- *1Cor6:12*

Your liberty to do all things does not make all things right, nor should anything enslave you. Any threat to what matters must be terminated before they terminate you and your purpose-driven living.

Chapter 3

Spending/Wasting Time

To improve the quality of your results in great measure, more time must be spent on the profitable and not just the pleasurable.

Although the idea of people running out of time reverberates everywhere, a review of how our day is spent reveals noticeable squandering of time on activities that add little value to our lives – things that feel good but hardly necessary or expedient. Because of these, we run short of time to do the really important things, leaving them usually at the mercy of pleasant irrelevancies.

For an assignment due submission, for example, most students do it at the dying minute; and while some of them take the time to do this assignment by themselves others simply wait to copy. Another class of students only realize on the day of submission that an assignment had been given and to catch up, they do the obvious – copy work or at best tardy work. The performance proclaims the amount of life focus wasted – a lot of below averages, abysmal failures, and a few marginal passes. If you tracked the students' activities before the deadline for time spent watching movies, playing video games, attending parties, idling around, and chitchatting, it would dawn on you that we are not dealing with dullards but simply with unfocussed students. About what mattered, they complained of having no time, sometimes incongruous: "We didn't come here only for studies, we have other things to do," the said other things being time wasters that can only engender profound feelings of shame and underachievement.

Away from the classroom and in offices, projects are not submitted on time because those assigned to them claim to have 'other things to do'. It can safely be said that most people fall short of realizing their goals because they get caught in the trap of doing the pleasurable rather than the necessary and profitable. People dodge or hurry home from work for no other employment than simply to sit and wind away time relaxed on a couch, swigging bottles of beer and/or watching movies and playing video games. So disproportionately lazy or unfocussed, when later in life hardship from unprofitable time usage comes to them, they miss the point and regard life as being unfair. We have enough time to do the really important things, which if left undone would undo us. We have ourselves to blame for letting time wasters eat up our true goals. What you put in is what you get out.

Knowing how doing the right thing today would impact the future, does one need to be coerced to map that future positively? Doing the right thing has to be seen from the right perspective, not as an anonymous activity benefiting others, but as a self-fulfilling objective expedient for the individual doer's future. It is obvious that without a deliberate choice to properly manage and use your time, you cannot amount to much.

Time Wasters

By their names we can tell what they are – the thieves of time and consequently of blossoming opportunities; the suppressors of dreams, passions, ideals, and goals. They cut deep into our time, producing little that can be considered meaningful. Consciously or unconsciously we spend time getting momentary satisfaction while losing a great deal in the
long run. While they last, the cheap glamour of tinsel satisfaction is considered to be just what we need; its promising pleasures and satisfaction seem to fill the vacuum in our bodies and souls. There we squander our time and receive fleeting amusement. Too soon, however, considerable regrets come to haunt our ageing life with failed or unrealized purposes. Oftentimes, it is then that we wake up to the reality that there were things we ought to have done, goals we ought to have pursued – pursuits that mattered but failed to do so. We chased

the shadow of passing gains and fleeting pleasures; we gave in and offered too much to time wasters.

We cannot waste time, we can only waste ourselves.

- *George Matthew Adams*

It is perhaps because of its abstract nature that we cheaply toss time off in bad bargains. Supposing time was money, would we be more careful with it? Would its constant supply debase its use in our esteem? Yet for illustration, let us consider that wasting 15 minutes of your time meant you would lose $500, it is convenient to think that we would be less willing to squander it unprofitably. But perhaps not, since all analogies are relative. What would constitute a waste of time differs from one service or professional objective to the other. "If you were in the entertainment industry, watching a film would not be wasting your time. If you were in the hospitality industry, checking out a new restaurant would not be wasting your time or money. The answer would be different for each of us. We all know when we are squandering time", to echo Donald Trump.

In effect, whenever you spend time on activities not related to your purpose, activities that do not help to make you better at who you are and what you do, you are wasting time. In bits and snippets, it might not be a call for concern, but when it becomes an occasional engagement of considerable amounts, precautionary measures ought to be invoked. It will be a waste of time for someone in the hospitality industry to sit for several hours a day watching films instead of going out to seek ways to make his or her industry better. Not many people would spend time studying, even for a couple of minutes and for their good, but they would chat with friends online or watch TV and play video games for hours unend. Not many entrepreneurs have the time to patiently sit and work out viable strategies on how to make their businesses more productive and profitable, but they can chat endlessly with a friend at a drinking hangout. Not many students love attending lectures, but they always seem to have more time than is required to go clubbing, partying, and joining social gatherings. They sideline or neglect activities of greater importance.

Time wasters add little to our life aspirations; they are unproductive interactions and indulgences, which although gratifying while they last, really offer little help to the dreams and visions we long to achieve. They derail our focus from the really important things. We must fend them off, for they are robbers that target our time along with the opportunity to materialize our dreams, our goals, and the meaning of our lives.

Dealing with Time Wasters

The acquisition of knowledge of the truth in any area of challenge in your life puts you in command in that area, and it is a truism that in every battle, vital knowledge about the enemy's strategies often contributes greatly to victory. Lack of knowledge of how the enemy operates often means an inability to effectively dismantle their stronghold. Knowledge in battle as in life is vital, in which respect, knowledge of time wasters exposes them to our overcoming, disabling, or even annihilation.

Common time wasters include:

1. Distractions
2. Procrastination
3. Lengthy thinking of the past
4. Living someone else's life
5. Unnecessary interruptions
6. Idleness and laziness
7. Unhealthy habits and emotions
8. We equally act as time-wasters to others due to our lack of punctuality.

Of these and many other wasters, the most significant and inclusive are distractions, procrastination, reliving the past, and trying to live other people's life. These will constitute the focal thrust of the next four chapters.

Key Points

1. You become what you invest your time in.
2. Sufficient time has been given to us to do the things which if left undone will ruin us.
3. We waste time whenever we prefer doing what feels good to what is important. When you spend quality time on activities not related to your life purpose, you are misusing it.
4. If you do not deliberately choose to manage your time well, you cannot amount to much
5. We cannot waste time, we can only waste ourselves.

Chapter 4

Distractions

Distractions are pleasurable deviations or digressions that frequently demand our attention with their primary motive being to take up time and prevent us from fully engaging in activities directly bound up with our life goals. They thus slow down the progress of really important issues. Sometimes they completely obtrude the beginnings of the value-imbued activities. One may view distractions as detention cells of time, energy, talents, and potential. The only difference is that they are often pleasurable and escapist in nature, offering fleeting relief, in exchange for large chunks of our time. We feel momentary 'good' while being lolled from perception and execution of ultimately better, more relevant, necessary, and important life issues.

Whatever prevents you from giving your full attention to activities that are of great value to your destiny is a distraction. Typically, watching a movie or playing video games is satisfying and good relaxation. The duration and timing, vis-a-vis dream-fulfilling activities, is where the problem resides.
And not only video/TV watching but engaging in spontaneous unproductive activities instead of paying attention to the task at hand is foolish. Craning for many passing things when you should be working equates to being distracted and so is partying when you should be studying, preparing for an exam, or being about a project. Anytime you give up on valuable activities or events for the sake of pleasures; or give up on studies or important tasks when they become challenging; or decide that it is 'boring' to be at your set task and switch on the TV, video or music or simply take up something else to 'pass time', you are simply entertaining distractions.

Even when boredom is not so addressed, we often too easily give up on completing certain important projects just because something seemingly thrilling pops up. Without a second thought, we switch activities – we pick up the phone to make a call or send a message that is not a pressing affair. Instead of completing important assignments or getting done with pertinent projects, we let ourselves get distracted by pleasurable attractions. The sad page comes later when an opportunity meets us unprepared. We do the Adam and Eve game of blaming others and circumstances, but not ourselves. The distractions you entertain will soon begin to define your life.

Some set good goals, but soon get deterred from commitment to them by giving in to distractions. The start is usually enthusiastic but with diminishing interest, they soon get snared by alternatives to the set goals, which for the most part do not deserve their quality time. The attraction of poorly timed activities is nothing less than a distraction. And there is none other to blame than ourselves. We are responsible for the shortcomings in attaining the plans we make. An inventory of our lives, identifying distractions, and adopting clearly defined principles on how to deal with them is the way out of the inertia of continued losses, failure, and mediocrity. Our doing far less than what we can do and ending our journeys way below the success mark ordained for us is a choice we make when we choose distractions, which have the power to do this. Entertaining distractions is the formula for below-average performance. It is rightfully referred to as "wasting time", a thing we need to wake up to.

Waking up to the value of time is perhaps the beginning of enlightenment and the shocking realization of the gravity of time wasting. Time is the substance of which life is fashioned, the fundamental resource needed to realize life dreams and ideas, birth life purposes, explore the wealth of our potential and creative abilities, and fulfil our divinely ordained life assignment. Robbed of time, we are simultaneously robbed of the opportunity to materialize all these.

Your results are the product of personal focus or personal distractions. The choice is yours.

- *John Di Lemme*

Compared to the hyped value of money, time is immeasurably valuable. Think of it. Is not the use of time to complete an important task, realize a goal or forge on with a plan to successful completion incomparable in the sense of satisfaction that results? It takes investing large amounts of time as well as other available resources to get there. Vis-à-vis this, we harp on watching movies, playing games, or chitchatting as emblems of typical time-wasting. But in moderation, none of these is wrong; they are relaxation which when poorly coordinated, overdone, or ill-timed, become counterproductive – constituting present pleasures but future hazards. Give work its due and complete the job before relaxation. And such relaxation should be measured in brevity, a stop-gap in-between purposeful and value-enhancing activities. This is to say that, though relaxation is essential, we must endeavour to choose the most effective means of renewal for anything that does not help us invest our time only helps us waste it.

Sources of Distractions

1. The mind

An untrained and undisciplined mind is a playground for shifting activities. Try to work on one project and just when you need to be most concentrated, your mind switches to something else, something more pleasurable or less demanding. The untrained mind is least cooperative at the early stages of a project. It quickly indicates that you are tired or need a break even when it's not the case. This is an escape route from the job at hand and the extra mile which any such job requires. The more demanding your goal, the more likely and urgent the mind suggests a switch. It plays other tricks, such as inducing self-doubt about your abilities relative to the blossoming of your projects, even though the very mind helped to fashion the ideas and framework of their implementation. In its creative versatility, the mind soon formulates alluring reasons for you to give up. And indeed the mind is the most effective manager of the destructive project.

Less Brown draws on a militarist image when he says: "if there is no enemy within, then the enemy without can do us no harm". The enemy in question is the untrained, undisciplined mind. From shifty flirtations through suggestions of your inability to carry on with the project on any excuse – you are not good enough, you don't have the right skill sets or qualifications, you are going to fail, and it is not worth your time. The untrained mind insists that your plans will not work.

It asks you the question, "If that idea is as good as you say it is, would it not have been discovered before now?"

This enemy in the house keeps telling you that others are better or smarter. If these others have not thought or effected such ideas, what makes you think you should or could? The defeatist mindset in essence is that because it was never done or thought of before, it is impossible. But that is the voice of the within luring you to spend time in your comfort zone. Believing such lies induces a fear-ridden existence and missing out on the fact that life starts outside the comfort zone. The good news is that with conscientious endeavour and adequate training, these destructive tendencies can be turned right around.

2. The Environment

The environment is a great input in life goal pursuits. The wrong environment foments wrong processes toward wrong results while the right environment helps towards the right results. As healthy fish thrive in good water and good seeds in good soil, so also is time, and consequently, our lives, when we are in a healthy environment, an environment conducive to development. The environment we live in and the people we interact with highly influence the way we spend our time. An environment full of distractions, for example, will only help waste our time while a favourable one eliminates distractions, helping us to maximize our time.

3. Unproductive Pleasures

Responding to every invitation to party or hangout, claiming to be enjoying life, when in fact you are only wasting it, is like being tossed about by every wind because you lack anchor or direction. Binge-watching the trendy, latest movies, listening to the latest hit songs, or playing the latest video games all fall under the category of time loss. This is not arguing for the need to be current about the goings on around on issues of great consequence to our lives, as they are equivalent to or closely associated with time spent in building up gifts, talents, and potentials to ensure our place among the successful.

The bane is wasting time on non-essentials when really important things ask for attention. Why kill time and self with the illusion of enjoying life when you can make better use of the time? It is bad economy to take up a less valuable option when better ones are available. Why not go for the position of a top achiever in your area of specialty rather than be stalled in inaction or meaningless activities? When will that long-incubated idea of yours – that song you always wanted to compose, the book you always wanted to write – feature to give meaning and serve as inspiration for others?

Paying attention to the external thrills of worldly pleasures is alienating ourselves from our ordained goal. The result is very predictable for we most certainly will wake up one morning to discover that we sacrificed our time for others and lost our purpose in life in the process. Prioritizing the pleasures of this world exposes us to being sucked dry of substance and heart-generated dreams. Instead of watching others, why not give a reason for others to watch and know you too? Let others too benefit from your talents.

4. Social Media

The place of social media on the time scale in today's generation shouts out. Android gadgets are excellent amenities to help us attain our goals faster and easier. But their abusive use enslaves and makes us psychopaths with fixations on passive and fruitless media activities. Societal assumptions play up to the destructive usage of phones and social media. The anonymous societal voice instils in us the law that if you are not by your phone when a call or message comes, you are being unconventional, rude, negligent, or even primitive. The phone is supposed to be a mobile gadget, you are told, despite the inherent hazards associated with this mobile imperative.

Away from the health hazards that professional health experts have adequately elaborated and enunciated about excessive mobile phone usage the phone and internet platforms are for convenience not for enslavement. If you, therefore, choose to allow others to harass you in your rooms, toilet, study, car, and everywhere else, it seems a silly and pathological choice. Then too, the content of the use of the phone begs to question; while valuable phone exchanges and educative online searches are invaluable, gratuitous chat and postings are into the category of distractions.

Consequences of Distractions

Distractions and Goals.

Distractions obstruct goal achievement. Getting distracted takes time, time that could be channelled toward accomplishing a goal. It takes time, diligence, and commitment to realize any task or indulge in distractive tendencies. When you choose to spend more time on one, the other suffers the effects considerably. Our earthly life is patterned on the following background:

Time wasters

Time, energy, finances and important resources

Our purpose, goals, aspirations, talents, potentials passions, ideas, vision, and mission

In the middle stands our time and other God-given resources for our enhancement via achieving our ordained purposes. Whether or not we get to the ordained future is up to us and how we employ the means at our disposal. Being willing, obedient, hardworking, and responsible, as well as tapping the ever-available divine assistance leads to the sure achievement of that goal. On the right are means and ends at our disposal, the mandate, and the ability for accomplishment. All we will ever dream of doing or becoming to be fulfilled lies within this bracket. The skills, unique talents, abilities, and gifts buried within each of us feature here. On the left are time wasters, offering no more than fleeting feelings of satisfaction.

Resources spilt out on distractions cannot be expected to guarantee life goals or dreams realizations for a certain mutuality holds time and different activity together so that doing more of one activity automatically means doing less of the other – perhaps what Jesus meant by declaring that you cannot serve two masters equally. Tasks are the masters you cannot serve at the same time with undivided attention. It is worse when the contrast between the masters is sharp for the effects of serving either of them manifest glaring differences of either success or failure. The polarized effects of distraction sharply differ from those of valuable concentration on worthwhile goals.

Distractions and Happiness

Happiness is realized in the process of fully utilizing our God-given potential. This makes success and profound happiness a function of purpose fulfilment, potential maximization, and goal accomplishment. Conversely, failing to reach our goals brings regrets and sorrow. So happiness is by distraction slaughtered on the altar of indulgence. Distractions take up the very time we need for the realization of dreams by pausing the process with temporary pleasure.

Distractions and Excellence

Not even the wretched appreciate goods and services of low quality and nowhere are below-standard products given premium rewards. Where an option is available, no one chooses substandard qualities. It requires little analysis to realize that we must gun for the highest quality. While the standards rise in our pursuit of the highest, we also at the same time maximize and deploy potential. This way, we affect God-ordained purpose to the success point of fulfilment and a life of abundance.

This success point is not jumped into by mere whim or thought process. It requires maturing and refining to be ready for consumption. Until then, our achievements are not ready for deployment yet. This process can be described as the honing of potentials and it takes time and focused effort to identify, cultivate, refine and polish these potentials. If you spend the time you ought to be refining your potential, or perfecting your skills, craft, or whatever drives your passion, on distractions, when will these skills be perfected? Whom will you blame if the opportunity, which is only a gift for the ready, meets you unprepared? The more we entertain distractions today, the higher the stakes and the greater the promise of a future life of mediocrity, lack, and want.

Distractions, Growth, and Potential

Until it matures and bears fruits and particularly when the fruits get ripe, a tree is hardly given much attention. It gets greater attention because it contains finished goods, goods in great demand. These fruits, which in principle were always there as part of the value of the source tree, blossom to view and make a difference. Potential, in like manner, becomes relevant only when it has been cultivated to maturity and finished utility.

Now, fruit trees don't carry their fruits to the market or force people to harvest them; the very fruits, when ripe, serve as invitations enough, as the saying goes, good wine needs no bush. When your talents are developed, you won't have to force people to notice you. Of course, this does not mean going out of your way to conceal your gift. With the right amount of exposure, the sheer iridescence of your fruits will be enough to bring you to notice. First, however, you must efficiently invest time, energy, and finance, to groom and perfect these abilities.

A man's gift well maximized will make room and sufficient provisions available for him, says the good book. The stakes are the distractions to avoid by putting in quality time to refine these potentials and ready them for deployment.

Distractions vis-à-vis Ideas and Productivity

When you are not investing in mind building, you are giving room for the depreciation of your mental faculties. Beyond low productivity, then, spending quality time on distractions engender a loss of stimulus, ideas, and gradual mental retardation. When the gnawing force of distraction touches on such root issues as mental capacity and eventual misuse of life and time, the need for painstaking application of methods to do away with them is no longer reasonably something to argue about.

Dealing with Distractions

There are perhaps as many sources of distraction as there are issues that distract. For some unified exposure, we here take them up in terms of mental, environmental, pleasurable, and social media distractions. No pretence is made of being exhaustive, however. The tendency of each distraction is pointed out and a suggested way out is indicated.

Mental Distractions

Concerning issues of the mind, we must work hard to keep our mind focused by training and feeding it with the right information to mould the right thoughts and ideas. The GIGO principle especially applies to the mind but beyond that, the mind can multiply what goes into its system. You can engage in mind-building and concentration exercises such as meditation, reading, and sometimes, absolute silence. However, these boosters can only be upheld in the ambience of self-discipline.

Self-discipline is probably the most important key to success in virtually every domain of life. It simply means developing the mental fortitude and drive, even in the face of overwhelming distractions, to do exactly what needs to be done when it needs to be done, and how it needs to be done. The desired results are to be your target, whether or not you feel like it. This is the key to efficiency and the secret of the success of many.

> *There is power in a clear, quiet, trained, disciplined, and focused mind, power to do virtually anything.*

Although commonly propagated, the attempt to control your thoughts or simply eliminate an undesirable thought pattern is not usually the solution. Thought patterns are like winds that come and go wherever there is a vacuum. To eliminate a thought pattern, rather than trying to create a mental vacuum, do its replacement with the one you consider necessary for the desired outcome. This calls for the deliberate choice of a thought line and stringent pursuit of it. The habit of flirting superficially with many ideas is useful only as a preliminary activity in brainstorming. Once the choice is made for a particular line of thought, pursue it with absolute thoroughness and to the end. Life does not favour mental instability. The expression 'mental instability' is a pathological reference to insanity. Therefore, allowing the mind to float and jump around carelessly, predicates mediocrity. Doggedness of course can be abusively used, but where it is based on sound calculation and choice, it only needs the willingness to make the necessary sacrifices and the individual will as sure as surety itself reach their desired goal.

There is power in a clear, quiet, trained, disciplined, and focused mind, power to do virtually anything. Training the mind is a challenging process but holds wonderful rewards for those who pull through with it. Persistence toward efficiency is also demanded for tasks. Pull in the mind to focus as exclusively on it as is reasonably possible till the project is completed. Submitting the mind to the will is disciplining it to wipe out performance mediocrity. In this regard, setting a time frame for the execution of important activities is a key component. Persistence and single-minded focus are the very essences of mental discipline, and when liaised with behaviour, actions, and habits, we obtain the formula for achievement.

Environmental Distractions

The most physical form of distraction is that of the environment and the solution is as direct as simply changing it. Some environments enhance and bring out our best in time management, concentration, and performance. Escape environmental distractions by finding and getting to the conducive one or by getting rid of the source of the distraction. While it may sound as radical as Jesus' figurative admonition that we get rid of our limb or eye if it causes us to sin, it should be said that if your TV set or some other gadget hinders you from concentrating, you might as well give it out temporarily, switch it off, or sell it off. In effect, a distracting TV does as much harm as a sin-causing limb or sensory organ.

If working in a room with a beautiful view outside the window distracts, move to one without a view. If studying at home is hampered by distractions, relocate elsewhere (to a school or prep centre) for better concentration.

In the category of environment, human presence can be brought in. If you find it difficult to study when your friends are around, make yourself available to them only outside your study hours. If you find it difficult to focus on the workload in front of you, without glancing at your phone after every beep, switch off the phone until work is over, or… get rid of it. Be gentle but astringent with yourself in this. Remember that these gadgets were created to help and not distract you. It's all about identifying a conducive environment that adds quality to your time and maximizes your usage. You are best able to identify the appropriate environment to bring out your best.

Particularly about environmental distractions, rather than fight them, avoid them by being at the right place at the right time for every given activity. We have already indicated the wisdom of getting rid of the source of distraction as well. This calls for self-knowledge of the things you can handle and the things you cannot, what works for you and what doesn't. There are people whose creativity blossoms in quiet and others who are inspired by activities. Late acclaimed Cameroonian novelist, A.T. Asong, for example, mapped his characters and plots from experiences at drinking spots. His example may indeed be an exception but vets the idea that there is no one perfect environment for everyone and everything. Concentrate on what works if it is the right thing to do and what doesn't work will fade into oblivion.

Whatever happens, vacate the environment that negatively influences your output. You do not need to entertain conversations you know are detrimental to your well-being. Take charge of your life as the clock ticks and time moves on whether you use it or not, whether you invest it or not, whether you make productive interactions with it or not. Time simply respects no one and waits for none.

Pleasures

Pleasure is a stimulant or spice of life. However, when transformed into a life purpose, it leads to destruction. That is why those who spend time trying to have it all, enjoy it all and experience it all here and now most certainly fall short of making it big time. The big mark of tomorrow is made through staying focused today, sticking to your goals, and refraining from the distracting pleasures of this world. With diligence and discipline, you can make it to the heights of achievement and from there have the opportunity to relax while making your contribution to the world.

Understanding the seasons or stages of your life and their demands is essential to your progress. While in the preparation season, it is wise to limit your outings and alone cultivate, refine, and polish the precious gems of greatness buried inside of you. That has been the wisdom and practice of all great achievers, among whom are renowned leaders. Biblical figures, including the prophets, Moses and Jesus Christ are known to have spent prolonged periods of aloneness before carrying out their great missions. While the recommendation would be ideal, you are at the very least required to spend more time doing those things you know draw you closer to your big dreams.

> *Understanding the seasons or stages of your life and their demands is essential to your progress*

Generally speaking, the internet, social media space, partying, and flitting engagements are distractors to be shunned, despite the pleasurable excitation they bring to you. Understand your season, and make the most of your time. Refusal to follow the crowd, if you don't want to, is the way to stand out and make a difference. It is the willingness to *"do today the things others won't do to have tomorrow the things they won't have,"* as Less Brown puts it. Refuse to be moved by those killing and wasting themselves away while claiming to be enjoying life. Choose to study while they party, to refine your talents while they chat or watch TV and 'enjoy' themselves unend. Choose the path of hard work while they waste away. Ultimately you will be making waves while they wail with regret. And that indeed is the simple way of growth, the way to stand out tomorrow and be counted; to be truly happy, you must be willing to pay the price today. Part of the price is sacrificing pleasures, enduring ridicule, being resource-conscious, and being different.

The seemingly good pleasures of the moment can wait while you work on your dreams. Distractions can wait while you make your contribution to the world. These distractions were there before you were born and pausing a while about their use is not going to be your death. Let them wait while you take the time to invest in yourself, a thing which if you do right now, will give you more leisure and means in the future to chat, party, and relax as much as you want. Let this be the time for planting and husbanding the seeds of greatness to maturity and eventual harvest. This is the time to work on your dreams.

Social Media

A lot that is of great use flows in the channels of social media and it is foolhardy to ignore this and lose out on the impressive stack of information therein. However, the passive nature of how social media information is absorbed adds up to curiosity, which has been described as aimless, endless and, useless. We cannot throw away the baby with the bathwater, but it cannot be denied that the media enslaves the user in a sort of addictive compulsory fixation to flirt from issue to issue purposelessly. The measure of learning should be purposefulness. For this reason, the two things to do about social media usage are:

1) For most people, limiting or minimalizing time spent on it

2) If you log into social media, be directed by a particular and clearly defined objective; limit yourself to achieving that objective and then simply sign out. Be wise, be ruthless with your time and dealings with others to make the most out of life.

Program your day

If you want to give your time to be used by others, the world will never run out of ways to make use of it and there are always pleasures at your disposal. The fact that we can do all things, as St. Paul says, does not make everything right to do. Naturally, there always will be people on social media but you cannot spend your entire life satisfying the demands of their presence. It is a matter of common sense that you are not obliged to respond to every notice on the social media platform, answer every call, or reply to every message. Following this, it is expedient to program certain hours during the day for attending to social media (important issues). At such times, you go online, do all you need to do, respond to relevant messages, make pressing calls, and, then sign out and continue your day. Your time is precious and once it gets used up, it never can be reclaimed. Be sure not to get it disproportionately used up on social media. This of course leaves out deliberate leisure, but centrally, your social media engagement should be purposive, even if that purpose is leisure, for leisure has its place in life.

Focus on Your Priorities

Give undivided attention to what you are at, avoiding distractions from others or other sources. Although there is an advantage to multi-tasking, mere distraction is often subtly difficult to tell apart from it. Focus often gets the job done better and quicker and so it is good to ensure that you get to set things done before moving over to others. In this way, there is cohesion and organic unity in your activities and the total effect of what you do. Whenever you feel a distraction lurking by, ask yourself this question: "Will what I am about to do be the best use of my time and energy at the moment?" If the answer is 'Yes', carry on; if not, refrain from it and proceed to what you know is important.

Distractions destroy action. If it's not moving you toward your purpose, leave it alone.

- Jermaine Riley

If we were willing to press the delete button of distractions, they would be dealt with once and for all. We only need to identify them and unsentimentally delete them. It is the best thing to do to time and better our life focus.

Key Points

- Just as attention is drawn to ripened fruits, so is talent in high demand when matured.
- Distractions take time, the same time that could be used for accomplishing goals.
- Self-discipline is probably the most important key to success in virtually every domain of life.
- There is power in a clear, quiet, trained, disciplined, and focused mind, power to do virtually anything.
- If you work now while others waste time, you will make your mark while they wail in regret. Understand your seasons and invest your time where it's most needed – on your craft.
- Relocate or press the delete button of distractions as soon as they pose a threat to all that matters to you and the attainment of your life goals.

Chapter 5

Procrastination

Procrastination is the bad habit of putting off until the day after tomorrow what should have been done the day before yesterday.

- Napoleon Hill

Procrastination is one limiting habit which must be properly dealt with if you hope to accomplish much in life. For one thing, it does not save time because we easily use the time we ought to have been using to fulfil the procrastinated task for what, in most cases, is of little importance. We use up the time derailed from the shelved activity unproductively. Thereafter, the chances of pushing that task further to the following day and the next increase. The remedy is that promptitude in purposive action must be upheld, which, it must be clarified, is different from rashness, as in quick unthinking, and poorly calculated action.

Causes of Procrastination

Procrastination is often due to discouragement or loss of enthusiasm, due to the supposed boring nature of the task. It is usually coloured by such drawbacks as indecision, disorganization, distractions, interruptions, and the frustrating or overwhelming nature of the task.

1. Discouragement

We easily tend to be discouraged and to get to immediate easier things when a task seems too challenging. The said task is then pushed forward to a later day and considered the ideal way out of the challenge. But that is not supported by results as remarkable strides and ground-breaking achievements in the world today are attained by men and women of determination, perseverance, and tenacity.

Instead of picking up a magazine to read or turning on the TV when challenged and discouraged, achievers put in more effort to see that their dreams and goals see the light of day. They stick on until the task is completed, despite having enough reasons to procrastinate or be distracted to eventually give up. Such are the people who understand the value of time and its relation to their life purpose; they understand the devastating negative consequences of procrastination.

Sometimes, procrastination or distractions seem to be a good substitute for complex or overwhelming exercises. The more they become increasingly complex, the greater the urge to digress to something less complex and more engaging. However, giving in to such desires is counterproductive because that fleeting pleasure or distraction will only lead to time wastage. The initial problem is not escaped by the waste of time. When you return to a procrastinated job, a thing you left just when you thought things couldn't get any worse, the problem might even then seem more complex than before. Besides, when you start all over, you still may get lured into postponing to a yet later date, thus continuing the cycle of waste.

No matter how discouraged we become, quitting the task at hand certainly does not get it done.

Reasons for procrastination abound since challenges are the very fabric of life. But we do not need to give in for no matter how discouraged we become, quitting the task at hand certainly does not get it done. It is best perhaps to make up your mind to stay on and get it done on time and properly. There is no positive argument for giving in to procrastination, besides laziness and distraction.

2. Side Attractions

Although discouragement from over-challenging tasks often induces procrastination, the turning point and motivation for its choice is more often the presence of other side attractions seeking our attention. Often these attractions are pleasurable by default. Such are options like giving up on studies or the completion of a project to binge-watch movies, play video games, or go on some other binging spree. Although these will always seem excellent, they are the short-term pleasures on an attractive platter for which the uncommitted fall rather than the task at hand which they describe as 'stressing up oneself'.

3. Waning Enthusiasm

Closely related to the discouragement from challenging tasks is waning enthusiasm, rather like the other side of the challenge. This does not often occur at the beginning but way into the task. It is easier to start than complete a project. So when gloomy days come, when the drive or motivation wanes, when nothing is moving as planned, when we run out of ideas and inspiration, when boredom or another form of spirit-breaking angst sets in, we are naturally tempted to give up. Such days are bound to come, but do we give up or push these tasks forward simply because we don't seem to have the drive to proceed with them? Should we abandon the initial carefully programmed task and yield to a passing hurdle?

Granted, programs are not unalterable or irreplaceable. If you have judged what you would want to replace the task you are currently working on to be more suitable, profitable, and beneficial at the moment, if what you are about to move into will give you better ideas or sufficient boost for the completion of the task being left uncompleted, then go right ahead and engage in the new task. This is way different from simply yielding to a feeling of disinterest in the task because of a distraction and a casual choice to push forward the completion of an activity to a later day for something less valuable. Although unnecessary stress on oneself is to be avoided, consistently sidelining a well-chosen life goal is to be considered distracting procrastination and misuse of time. The recommended solution is to accomplish what matters at that moment, irrespective of dissuading feelings. Sheer grit is sometimes the only thing of value in our gamut of choices. But as already indicated, giving yourself meaningful respite or relaxation is not a taboo, so long as it enables you to better focus. It is over-stretching or turning such a respite into a full-time engagement that is frowned upon. Focal intent on a task is beyond fine feeling; it is a deliberate choice.

4. Indecision

There are times when decision-making can be frustrating. Not knowing what to do or how to go about a thing can be even worse than knowing what to do and not knowing how to get it going. Indecision in itself is a cogent force for procrastination; the task we are undecided on how to do is easily substituted for activities that float to us needing no definite choice or decision. You do not need to decide whether or not to get distracted, it is a default choice that is never frustrating or overwhelming, but spontaneous, popping up in our minds whenever a current engagement proves challenging.

Faced with situations vital to shaping our future, we are likely to make true decisions. Faced with a life-and-death scenario, true decisions are made. Although postponing such a decision may be seasonally attractive, failing to promptly decide leaves time to decide for you. The options in that do not quite favour you because time's choices are random and sometimes unfavourable. It is perhaps best to face the music of a hard choice. Sit down, relax, and with a rational mind, decide on what needs to be done. Make a choice today and stand on it so that tomorrow comes with predictable outcomes for you related to your deliberate choice.

Waiting hurts; forgetting hurts, but not knowing which decision to take can sometimes be the most painful [and utterly frustrating]

- Jose N. Harris

Overall, procrastination kills time, limits the maximization of potential, and, in the long term, frustrates the possibility of you realizing your life goals. It leads to the loss of opportunities brought on by the incompletion of already stacked activities. It thus obstructs productivity as it pushes valuable tasks to the background and foregrounds mediocrity. This is myopia and loss of vision which in turn destroys enthusiasm. Since ideas tend to grow or flow as they are put into action, pushing forward activities flags not only enthusiasm but the source impetus of ideas. The flagged thought erases impetus and grounds the procrastinated task. The motivation for the start of the task becomes too blurred for a retake, refocus, or completion. No wonder then that an eternal cycle of postponement continues with the impetus of procrastination inertia and scatters in its wake countless uncompleted big or small projects. That is how forcefully procrastination erupts as a killer of dreams, ideas, and goals. It is not only the thief of time, but also of everything precious in between. Only a retaliatory response can rescue and resurrect tasks and aspirations from such a snare.

Every Moment Counts

Time moves on and procrastination lays an extra burden on the already busy day of tomorrow. Piling up more activities for 'someday' lays up mounds of discouragement and eventual giving up on prospects even when the time is ripe. Procrastination is thus a signal of low self-value, and indifference to our dreams, ideas, time, and future. The way out is to act now.

Dealing with Procrastination

Find something to do or complete what you were already working on. You do not need to be great or to have the resources needed before you start. If you do not start somewhere with just what is available, you will hardly reach any greatness or even accumulate the needed resources. Start with your inspired action now and stick to it. Promptness is one mark of achievers.

If you wait until the wind and the weather are just right, you will never sow anything and never harvest anything.

- *Ecclesiastes11:4_GNT*

By sheer wisdom of experience, my mother always reminded me not to start up with new tasks until I had completed the already started one. She would also warn me not to prolong completion of one thing because in so doing, I might miss other opportunities or get mix-ups regarding future projects. Because every moment is crucial in the realization of life goals, it is recommended that one does something each day toward it. Although you don't need to be great before you start, you, however, must start – somewhere and with what you have, to be great someday. As much as possible, the necessary things should be done properly and on time. Incomplete projects are not to be left around for they are like binding ropes that keep one back from progressing. And not only suspending a project but protracting its execution also has its drawbacks, particularly loss of interest and eventual abandonment. Time consciousness is thus necessary; a proportionate time allocation for activities on hand is necessary.

This takes us back to the notion that action should be based on decisions rather than emotions. You do not need to feel like doing something before engaging to do it, and you do not protract or hold on to one activity just perhaps because it is more pleasurable. And the argument that some necessary activities might not pose themselves in the best of conditions for execution is true. Yet waiting for perfect conditions is not the recommended choice. The recommendation is for you to simply take the plunge. Being fully informed of what needs to be done, just get going. It is this discipline to do, to act despite waning enthusiasm, boredom, or the alluring deceptions of side attractions, that defeats procrastination.

The sooner you take action to complete the said task, the better you are enabled to move to the next activity with nothing to hold you back. The discipline of getting things done on time is very enabling and contributes to a stress-free life. In other words, taking prompt action and getting things done, not prompted by feelings, but by choice, clears what is imagistically referred to as your dirty backyard and with it the knots that contort your life.

1. Love what you do

Love is a motivating factor that keeps enthusiasm burning always. It wipes out discouragements and keeps you focused, refreshing your strength even when the task at hand seems challenging. Loving what you do or doing what you love, puts you at your best. Love here does not mean a cozy feeling, but a decisive choice that affirms the goodness and worthwhileness of the action you are at.

2. Start from the End Goal

One way of stirring up your interest is previewing the consequences of completing or not completing the said task on time. You could fail your end-of-year exams if you don't study hard. You could lose your job, if you fail to submit that project or complete the assignment your employer gave you. This is negative motivation as it were but valuable. If it fans your drive, fair and good. Efficient use or waste of your time depends on what you choose to fan when you get discouraged. The original intention and envisaged glamour of success, the previewed feeling of fulfilment at the thought of completing your task, the impact of your accomplishments on the lives of others …You could also revert to these and be boosted to action. If these do not raise your spirits enough, find something or some other reason to encourage yourself. You are responsible for your life and future and all that goes on in it. Since you are to bear the consequences of your actions too, it is necessary for you to do what it takes to be boosted and to feel rewarded for the value of your work to you and society.

One major reason for failure in life is the mindset of inability, the attitude that predicates failure; 'I can't make it'. No wonder the humming reverberation of Barack Obama's campaign slogan went the rounds of the world: "Yes we can". A simple phrase but with telling power. The expression comes against the background of defeatism widespread among the vast majority of humanity who tell themselves that they are not good enough or that their work does not amount to anything worthwhile. The "I can't" view, of course, is counter-productive.

3. Prioritize

Efficient time management is eased by prioritizing. Your ability to organize your tasks in order of importance saves time, eliminates frustration, and gives you that sense of direction.

I noticed later on in my life that anytime I said; "I will do it tomorrow", I was procrastinating – at least 90% of the time. A close examination of what I was currently doing, or the nature of the activities I had programmed for that day, served as added proof of that. If you objectively analyze what you are considering trading that important task with, perhaps you will come to the same conclusion – sufficient time has been made available today and every other day. Your choices of activities are just not the best. Prioritization is really about reasonable work organization, in this context.

4. Concentrate

Concentration enhances self-discipline and helps fight procrastination. Concentration is aided by the ability to view your work as a complete pack, refusing to be taken off it till it is completed. Concentration itself generates ideas and the equipage to facilitate the completion of the given task. Experience shows that when one loses concentration, it becomes easy to miss out on ideas and the overall process. In turn, losing out on ideas may make procrastination a possible choice.

Once you have begun a task, think of the completion in terms of a series of stages and get done with each step before moving to the next. Disorganized tackling of a job is no help, although if you judge a particular activity as more important, you could allocate more quality time to ensure its completion. Whatever the situation, however, do not let your task be over-drawn out for then it becomes easier to lose your focus. Where there is the will, the way can be found. Concentration enhances this process, opening up doors to ideas and resources instrumental to the completion of the task at hand –

resources and ideas that stay hidden from those who are constantly adrift. This way, concentration speeds up action and defeats procrastination. Concentrate on your priorities and everything else will fall in place.

The 'Tomorrow Syndrome'

Tomorrow is the only day of the year that appeals to a lazy man who thinks anything can be done anytime. But what may be done any time, really will not be done sometime. For this reason, it is important to set goals and make things happen when they ought to. This not only spares you the stress and frustration of tomorrow but gives a notching of achievement and a sense of growth piecemeal.

---

*Whatever you think you can do or believe you can do, begin it
[as soon as possible]. [Concise and Precise] Action has
magic, grace and power in it.*

– Johann Wolfgang Von Goethe

The things usually held over for another time are the things we do not feel like doing. But these are the things that need to be done and the time we don't feel like doing them, is often the ideal time to get them done. It is therefore imperative that we adopt a prompt and proactive approach to appropriate action, not pushing action to another day – tomorrow. Tomorrow already has enough activities to take care of. Act now so you can use tomorrow's time for something better. This counters one of the attractions of procrastination – the assumption that tomorrow will be less choked up. But unexpected schedules often make tomorrow even busier than today.

Key Points

1. What may be done at 'anytime' will be done at no time.
2. Time will pass, whether we put it to use or not. We may delay, but time will not! (Benjamin Franklin).
3. For time to be efficiently used, it must be dutifully spent on maximizing our core life priorities.
4. When you start, be sure to complete it.
5. One way of stirring up your interest is previewing the consequences, or rewards, of completing or not completing the said task on time.
6. Successful people do today what wishful thinkers plan on starting someday.

Chapter 6

Dwelling on the Past

Remember ye, not the former things, neither consider the things of old. Behold, I will do a new thing; now it shall spring forth; shall ye not know it? I will even make a way in the wilderness, and rivers in the desert.

- *Isaiah 43:18, 19*

It is not uncommon for people to spend huge amounts of time going through memories – past mistakes, past successes, holding on to painful experiences and regrets. However, it is not wise to live life always looking backwards. The past ought to be left there since it never will be altered. Although the past makes us who we are today, it is not supposed to be a burden. Its closed door should not keep us from beholding the gate that has been opened ahead of us. It has been beautifully put in an anonymous write-up that we are to consider our past a waste paper; the present, a newspaper, and the future a question paper. Come out of your past, control the present, and make your future what you want. You are not what happened to you but what you choose to become. Whom you can become will only be made possible by how you choose to spend the resources now at your disposal.

What happened yesterday is irreversible history. It is the one thing you have no control over anymore, so dwelling on it is counterproductive. It is worse if the said experience was a bad one because hurt and regret would be dredged up to ruin the present. The mistakes of yesterday can only be regretted, not undone. While the lessons learnt can indeed help towards a better today and brighter tomorrow, incessantly holding on can be detrimental. Holding on to yesterday is like driving forward and looking backwards, like having your hands on the forward-cutting plough and looking back all the time.

It is hard to fully pursue your path unless you stop looking back at what you think you might have lost. Driving through life fixated on the rear mirror of what is past rather than paying attention to the path you should be blazing is unconventional and less likely to be a successful scheme. Past mistakes, failures or even achievements must not be allowed to prevent you from new possibilities and future frontiers. Live in the moment and work for your future. We are to use or build on our past, making it a springboard rather than fruitlessly dwelling on it.

Akin to preoccupation with the past is mental idleness, thinking nothing serious or focal vacuum. Hours go by, simply wasted in vacant nothingness or daydreaming. We must make that conscious decision to mentally and physically be anchored to definitive action and make the most of the now. Instead of obsessively holding on to what can't be undone, our time now can be put to more productive use by choosing to prepare ourselves and our inherent gifts for future use. You cannot change your past, but there is still so much you can do, starting today, and now, to make your future better – better than what you wished your past had been. Refuse, therefore, to put the past in the obtruding path of the present; fashion your thoughts into constructive strands of focus and effective purpose. Maximize the present; refuse to leave it at the mercy of your past or vagueness.

Time Waste Effects

1. Kills time and limits opportunities

Maturing and maximizing potential takes time. When potential is not maximized, opportunity cannot be maximized. When an opportunity is not maximized, a sequence of grief and regret is unleashed. Since we cannot see far ahead, we need to watch out for opportunities. But many people let opportunities pass them by refusing to own up to their past mistakes or by spending time morosely thinking of the said mistakes along with the unused or lost opportunities. This way, they lose sight of what is ahead of them. The moment you revert to and dwell long enough on the past, you miss out on what is right in front of you.

Holding on to past experiences rather than changing strategies and adapting to changing times is foolish. Resting on one's laurels is just as corrosive. The past of any hue induces high levels of fear and pessimism, on the one hand, and presumptiveness, on the other hand. Except for the lessons they stand to teach us, the past is to be reasonably shunned. But above all, the negative past must be buried. Most of those who venture there tend to unearth the mistakes they made and things they failed to do, plunging themselves into regret, and hurt thereby.

Remorseful dwelling in the negative past is weeping over spilt milk – a useless and harmful activity. Wallowing in past mistakes prevents us from basking in the joy and satisfaction available in the opportunities which lie about and ahead of us. New doors have been opened to you, but until you decide to stop looking intently at the shut doors, you are bound to lose more and weep even more later. The best way to get over past hurts is to invest in future happiness, which requires cutting the hold of the limiting pasts and looking to the future where the seeds of possibilities lie.

2. Prevents making the most of life and potential

While shutting the doors to the future, being stuck in the past defeats self-fulfilment. It misses out on the fact that there is much more to life than what we miss or fail to do. The plenitude of opportunities must not be sacrificed on the altar of regret. It must be remembered that the world needs our contributions to its well-being way beyond and far out of our narrow ruts of past mistakes. We must burst forth with the decisiveness to live life to its full.

If it is any consolation, everyone has a past. Biblical figures who should have been frustrated by dwelling on their past but who brushed it aside and faced their destinies are many by the count. Peter (Mtt 26:69-75) blundered grievously and many times. Paul had to make a total turnaround from a persecutor to a preacher: forgetting the past, he forged forward for the prize. David too, his adultery and murder should have held him back, but no. Almost every significant biblical figure, including Abraham, Jacob and Moses had something seriously negative against them and which could have held them back, but they did not dwell on those negative thoughts. The same can be said of quite a handful of today's success stories. Many of them will attest to having gone through experiences that could completely shut them down, and blind them from any hopes of a bright future. Some will attest to having been abused, while the multiple losses and failed attempts of others will be nothing if not shocking. Yet, these served as motivation to strive for something better, to make a mark on the earth, and to impact lives through their encounters. We all have missed out on some valuable life opportunities, and relationships. If others were able to move on, you can too.

It is not asking too much of us to forget the past and forge ahead since that is the only way to fulfil our life purpose or God-destined goals. Looking over your shoulder at what could have been, clinging to what is already gone by or attempting to pull back the receded past is an error. There is of course a difference between taking an inventory of the past and dwelling on the past. An inventory is a healthy and highly recommended habit that helps to keep a check on your life and to monitor its overall progress relative to your life goals. However, brooding on lost opportunities that only serve as traps that bind one in darkness away from the light of the new day is something else.

It doesn't matter what happened yesterday or the circumstances surrounding your birth or your life; it doesn't matter what somebody told you or the hurting experience you had or what might have led to great success. It doesn't matter how bad or comfortable your past may have been. The mistakes you made the errors you committed, the people you hurt – that is past; lengthy thinking on them does not solve or better the situation. Just as you would not kill yourself because of your errors, shut down on life and keep living in the past, it is unwise to hold yourself interminably to blame. Closing up on life, backing out on the pursuits of the dreams you once cherished – these do not salvage anything. For the past cannot be redone, but assuming that the best is yet to come, liberates you to catch the moment and with it the future.

The robbers of time are the past and the future. Man should bless the past, and forget it if it keeps him in bondage, and bless the future, knowing it has in store for him endless joys, but live fully in the now.

- Florence Scovel Shinn

Past successes also register as threats to future success because they create a mood of presumptive assurance that makes us lose the mental alertness that is a prerequisite for concentration, effectiveness, and advancement. A season that has already ended, no matter how good, memorable or painful it may have been, is gone and out. It is best to enter the new season unhampered. In entering the new season, be willing to let go of what you lost or gained.

Yesterday has to be seen as a myth in memory, tomorrow a mystery and today a gift. The myth should not obstruct quality time with the gift which hopes to unravel the mystery. It is in the present that you must live and in it find something important to do towards your visualized future. In the process, refuse to dwell on past hurts as you forge ahead, properly charting out the course to attain what you hope will be. The backbone of such a process is a life vision and a firm resolve to be at it by shunning idleness:

A life vision

A life vision is a vivid mental picture of what you want your future to look like; where you would love to be, what you would love to achieve or have and who you would love to become. It is a way of moving forward; of letting go of what was and making use of what now is, to make the most of what still can be. For this vision, adopt the necessary and suitable plans needed to attain the anticipated future. Vision connotes looking with the eyes of your imagination into the future God has ordained for you. This vision births the need to come up with plans on how to cause its full realization. Having plans generates the urgency to set goals. It is through the set goals that the diligent worker, wasting no time on the past, stretches himself to attain the great heights yet attainable.

With vision being future-focused, the man with a vision has little time to spend on past events. Such a one focuses on the best of his or her ability and ordained goal. A vision, this way, starves the obnoxious habit of fixation on particularly the negative past, although, as indicated elsewhere, the positive past too has its pitfalls.

Shun idleness.

The wandering mind often feeds on the past, a default staple. Refuse to be trapped that way and take up proactively designed activities that bear on your future. This is a choice of busy efficiency as opposed to just being busy. It is being busy with current and profitable activities, making the most of the moment. In this application to the present, life naturally will chart the right course for you to arrive at your destined future.

Key Points

1. Life is a forward march with the past as the springboard, not a lounging bed.
2. The past is a wastepaper; the present is a newspaper, and your future is a question paper, a blank sheet whose content you get to decide.
3. It is unwise to dwell on what could have, should have or would have been. Focus on what is and what you now have while charting out a course for what you hope will and can be.
4. Let go; have a clear vision and shun idleness.

Chapter 7

Another Person's Life

Trying or desiring to be others, doing things their way and not your way, hankering for their talents and undermining your uniqueness and peculiarity is a frustrating venture. One mark of blindness to the fact that we all have different shoe sizes is the struggle to fit into the shoes of others. Trying to master the dance steps of others while ignoring the rhythm ordained for you is foolish. Created differently, with distinct sets of potentials and desires, we should each follow our distinct path in life, not living others' lives. Doing what you were not called to do is not only burdensome and ineffective but irrelevant. Your task is to identify where and what you are called to serve and then engage it thoroughly.

Each path, no matter how big or small, popular or unpopular, significant or insignificant it may appear to be, not only glorifies God but also fits perfectly into his grand scheme and master plan. It also exalts the one who diligently functions at that level, serving as an avenue for the maximization of imbued talents or potentials.

This is not vilifying strategic emulation or trying to get to the heights of another person whom we consider to be our model. Far from it. If others inspire and uplift us, we should echo. The only reservation is that we must do so only to accentuate our inbuilt talents. We are considered genuine only to the extent that we tap from our inner selves without prejudices to those who inspire us.

On the other hand, trying to live a borrowed life means missing the right path and taking the wrong direction headed for a destination that was never meant for you. It leads to failure and unnecessary struggle in trying to play another's role. Other negative consequences naturally flow from this, including negative comparisons, and competing with others, rather than evaluating success in terms of one's set goals and the best one could be. Overstretched by doubling efforts to reach a mark they were never built for, the imitator of another's life ends up frustrated and unfulfilled. He or she mistakes the neighbour's greener pastures for level ground and plunges into doom. Overall, the ambience of imitating others is blanketed by jealousy and envy whose bleak signs develop, creating a whorl of vicious and concentric negative cycles. This must not be.

1. Be yourself and identify your ordained path

Keep up with heaven's rhythm rather than that of your companions. Our destinations are not only different but each is unique. We are therefore never tied to anyone, much less the route they are taking to fulfil their destinies. Our best bet is to stick to the heaven-mapped route, timing, purpose and vision for our life.

Not everyone is called to be a music artist, ballplayer or movie star. By the way, who was born already a star? No one. Stars are not born stars but identify where they are called to function and then diligently and patiently apply themselves to it. The rest is the result. As it were, God exalts them from handling small to big things. Each got an initial investment that would be nursed to make them great. These seed traits are individual uniqueness – our uniqueness. If everyone were to play ball or be a movie actor, there certainly would be no entrepreneurs, teachers, scientists, leaders, pastors, farmers or researchers in the world. If we would all be writers, what would happen to singing, drama, painting and even comedy?

On the private individual plane, you only need to identify with heaven's timing, rhythm and route for your life and what unique gifts and talents God has endowed you with. That is the path ordained for you and you only need to be diligent there where relevant resources have been stationed for your optimal best. Along that path, you are relevant and provided with a means to make it great in life, attain happiness and in the process, glorify God.

If a man loses pace with his companions, perhaps it is because he hears a different drummer. Let him step to the music which he hears however measured or far away.

-   Henry De Roe

Your significance is not in similarity to others but in your uniqueness, point of difference or even oddness. That is what places you as the number one, the first in a unique trend. Let others be the best they were created to be; yours is to work at being the best 'you' possibly can be. The real 'you' is an overall successful and happy you. Only do not be scared or let your present circumstances shirk your resolve to scale the heights. As God's child, your future couldn't be brighter and more glamorous as it has been ordained. Let God then be true and let every man or circumstance or situation or experience be a lie; for His plans for you are of prosperity. The snag is that it will only come when you identify and accept to work with and as the real you; when you choose to appreciate and value your uniqueness.

For all, the rise to greatness evolves from working at being the best they were called to be and not in trying to be like others. Uniqueness and single-minded application to a clear vision are what significantly moved and propelled civilization forward. You are allowed to have mentors or models, people you admire, love to learn from and would want to obtain the results they are obtaining, but true results cannot be from negation or in giving up on your uniqueness. Only use the success principles of others to build and refine your unique qualities. This is why it can truly be said that greatness comes from within and authenticity is the path to genuine achievement. There is a place for the real you at the top. What you carry, who you are, matters.

2. Your Strengths

Integrity, authenticity or being true to the self are expressions that capture the genuineness that makes for true growth. This genuineness shows up in your gifts, talents, skills and abilities being well refined and maximized. This showing up or forth is the process of making room for you at the top, causing you to stand before kings and great men. It is on the inside, the skills, talents, gifts and creative abilities buried within you that, like a seed, you evolve. Yours is to build, refine, polish, upgrade and deploy them when they get ready.

Gold, precious stones and minerals are usually found deep in the earth. The rich treasure deposits of potentials stored up within us, by analogy, are also deep within. No precious stone carelessly lies on the surface of the earth. To get them, we must dig deep into the earth. Every valuable thing found within us is deep down. Deep within each of us is the rich store of treasures God has placed in us.

The world being a busy place, we can get caught up in its haste, especially when we focus too much attention on what the world is doing or how it is operating. So distracted, we hardly take the time to look within for what we could pull out to contribute to the evolving world. So we peer about and crane for novelty and details of the world, a thing which is rather limiting. We do not need that externalization since all we need to live a fulfilling, rewarding, impactful, successful, contributive and happy life is richly buried within us.

Sadly, many people miss out on their talents and the rich treasures within them by attempting to fit into the ways of others and the world rather than plant, cultivate and fertilize their distinct treasures. Value yourself, your passion, your dreams, desires and talents; hold them in high esteem and make them soar to greater heights. Desire to be better than you were yesterday, making adequate use of the time you have now. Maximize your strengths (your gifts); they have been designed to make room for you at the top.

Key Points

1. Your significance is not in similarity but in difference and uniqueness from others.
2. There is a divine reason for your gifts, abilities, and inclinations. God makes no mistakes.
3. Things of value don't carelessly lie on the surface; we need to dig deep to find them.
4. Single-minded purposefulness is vital to happiness.
5. Every seed carries its unique tree. Your way to affluence is within you already.

Chapter 8

Unhealthy Habits and Emotions

What you permit increases; what you allow grows; what you compromise with only gains more grounds

Some habits and emotions are delimiting, keeping us bound and unable to freely embrace life. They kill time by holding us down wastefully to things we are unable to change. We are soon tempted to give up what matters and our dreams and future are blurred, look bleak and unreachable. Typically, guilt, depression, self-pity, worry, fear, anxiety, a bad temper as well as bitterness have these effects on us. They are the emotional arm of the limiting habits already discussed – laziness, procrastination, excessive sleeping and sluggishness.

Guilt, Depression and Self-Pity

Guilt is worry or unhappiness that is due to an unwanted deed, usually something bad or wrong, which causes displeasure or harm to another person. The guilty person tends to yield to depression which is liaised to hopeless unhappiness. In turn, this brings about self-pity. This latter is implosive sadness brought on by a conviction that one has too many problems or has suffered a lot.

Guilt, depression, and self-pity are a progression that reveals a state of a man trapped along with his time and dreams in unproductivity. The victim, absurdly, seeks comfort in negativity, hopelessness and unhappy feelings. This stalls the victim in extreme sadness as the cloud of past mistakes blankets and binds his/her prospects.

Staying in guilt is not only suppressive but lethal to time and life. A mindset of self-blame is devastatingly crippling and self-poisoning. Guilt prevents the victim from finding reason to forgive the self and in the progression from guilt through depression to self-pity, even sanity can be lost. The overwhelming effects of negative emotions can go that far. As guilt drains the life of the person, it instils pain, regret, depression and frustration. From losing their drive in life, some resort to suicide. No one needs these for any purpose and certainly not for progress in life.

Negative emotions must be seen as highly destructive viruses that cause the malfunctioning of the reasoning faculties as they prevent fresh thoughts and constrain the guilty to perpetually relive past failures or mistakes. The nest of negativity is infested with a general atmosphere of despair, but the victim needs little more than the decision to break free and move on. Four simple steps are suggested by many:

1. Admit your faults

Refusing to accept responsibility for our mistakes will keep us from apologizing or asking for forgiveness from those we have hurt. Admitting your mistakes, and apologizing doesn't make you weak or soft as is often interpreted; on the contrary, it is a sign of maturity and a necessary element to tangible progress.

2. Ask for forgiveness

From God and from those our actions have hurt. Beyond hurting individuals and ourselves, we hurt the owner of the world and it is to Him we should direct our first apology. Ignorance of this keeps many in perpetual guilt, despite the express declaration in His word; *"I, even I, am he that blotteth out thy transgressions for mine own sake, and will not remember thy sins." (Isaiah 43:25).*

If we humble ourselves and turn to God, He is willing to forgive. While it may not be put on show for all to see, Divine forgiveness is vital. Through it comes the peace of God, in the absence of which no happiness or progress is possible. Genuine and deliberately expressed remorse towards the Divine Being is a way to restore the connection with the stabilizing source and director of all things. If staying in guilt kills time and joy, living a guilt-free life builds life, true success and progress.

And then... Forgive Yourself

Even after God has forgiven you, you need to forgive yourself. Wallowing in painful memories of mistakes or failures is indicative of a lack of self-forgiveness. This cannot be a godly action since fulfilling your destiny is God's will. What holds an individual back from his or her best cannot be God's will for them.

3. Move on

When you finally admit your mistakes, apologize and ask for forgiveness, you will be freed from the burden of guilt and regret. However, moving on is the decisive fourth and final step to breaking free from the limitation of guilt. Even when forgiven by God and by those they hurt and even by themselves, some people cling to the draining force of stagnation, unable to move on along the path they were ordained to take. Moving on is the direct opposite of dwelling in the cage of guilt feelings and negativity. It is a courageous and cheerful engagement in life in the spirit of someone sure to succeed. The best is still to come, but until you invest time in the forward thrust towards that best, it will never become your reality.

Fear, Worry and Anxiety

To be worried means to think about problems or unpleasant things that might happen in a way that makes you feel unpleasant and frightened. It is the quandary of expecting things to not work out for good, and at the same time feebly hoping that you are wrong in that negative expectation. This puts the individual in a state of unrest. Feeding your mind with negative expectations gives it a reason not to stay calm or function properly. You are hardly able to do something or think of something else as these emotions create great internal and sometimes external instability.

They hold you back from your best, confiscating the time that could be used for productivity. As with the group that culminates in depression, these emotional drains can also be tackled in three moves:

Believe God and his word.

In response to emotions of fear, worry and anxiety he says:

Do not fret or have any anxiety about anything, but in every circumstance and in everything, by prayer and petition (definite requests), with thanksgiving, continue to make your wants known to God.

And God's peace [shall be yours, that tranquil state of a soul assured of its salvation through Christ, and so fearing nothing from God and being content with its earthly lot of whatever sort that is, that peace] which transcends all understanding shall garrison and mount guard over your hearts and minds in Christ Jesus. (Philippians 4: 6, 7 AMP)

The Message Translation of the Bible puts it this way:

Don't fret or worry. Instead of worrying, pray. Let petitions and praises shape your worries into prayers, letting God know your concerns. Before you know it, a sense of God's wholeness, everything coming together for good, will come and settle you down.

In Proverbs 3:25, 26 we read: *"Be not afraid of sudden fear, neither of the desolation of the wicked when it cometh. For the Lord shall keep thy foot from being taken"*

Overall, we are enjoined to have no fear, worry or anxiety, but to present our petitions to Him who promises never to abandon us or let us go astray. It is then a wholesome thing to let God take over, to let His peace rule our hearts. Peace of heart is the elixir of life and without which we cannot be our best. The recommendation then is for us to slough off the worry that entraps and causes us to use our time unproductively. By contrast, a peaceful mind releases and opens us up to opportunities about us.

Negative emotions are not invincible but when allowed to dominate, they seem so. Having faith rather than yielding to fear, presenting our requests to God, rather than being anxious dissolves them.

Expect the best

Expectations can bring peace or anxiety. For the most part, we do not expect things to work out well, and this keeps us in fear. We remain captives of negative emotions which rip us of valuable time in which we could be more productive. In practice, positive expectation means that when fear creeps in, we reassure ourselves by saying: "all will be fine," that we shall make it to the victorious finish. Good things can happen to you too, believe and expect that. Be positive, and always expect the best. This will help you rid yourself of negative emotions.

Good things can, and are supposed to happen to you too.

Be faith-filled

Telling yourself things won't work out is the easiest way to make sure they don't. Being fear-filled, worry-filled, anxiety-filled and depression-filled always produce negative results. However, it is as easy to make negative declarations as it is to make positive ones – and depending on the actions that follow, both have the same likelihood of materializing. The choice is not between a difficult pronouncement and an easy one but between virtual equals. The difference is simply one of choice. Tell yourself things are going to work, that everything will work out fine, and that with the right course of action, they will.

The confession principle is based on the observed fact that the words we speak have tremendous power; that our thoughts and words shape our actions – they should, and our actions shape our lives. We should then refuse to fear, to be worried or to be anxious. We can do this by prayer through which we can take hold of God's peace and insights made available for all. By faith-induced confessions, we break free and move on. Practical faith is therefore the effective way to deal with negative emotions.

We all go through rough times at some point in our lives. They are almost unavoidable. However, how we react to them is up to us. You can choose to engage in unhealthy habits with the excuse that you are trying to cope with a bad break or engage in productive remedies to your predicament. At the end of the day, though, nature will reward you based on your actions and not your intentions or excuses, no matter how convincing they might be.

Joel Osteen likens our lives to containers that can take only a specified volume of liquid. Whatever gets into it, takes up a fraction of the volume of the container, reducing how much it can take. If we let guilt, worry, anger, depression, fear, anxiety and self-pity take up valuable space in these containers, we soon run out of space for joy, peace, and good health. If we occupy our time containers with negative emotions and bad habits, we soon run out of time for the things that add meaning to life.

Key Points

1. Time wasters such as distractions, procrastination, dwelling on the past, idleness, and laziness, cut deep into our time, producing little benefits.
2. Getting robbed of time cuts our chances of realizing our life goals.
3. Pursuits, activities, habits, or ventures that don't help us accomplish our life goals, dreams, and aspirations are resource wasters and threats to pursuits that matter. The sooner you deal with them, the safer your time and resources will be.
4. Your destiny is not in your similarity to others but in your point of difference from them.
5. Our habits and emotions should help us to maximize our time and not the other way around. Therefore, eschew all negative usage.
6. Dwelling on guilt, worry, fear, anxiety, depression, self-pity, low self-esteem and even past successes and memories threatens your today and the future.
7. Forgive yourself and move on to become a better person and of better service to others.

Part Three

Time Consumers

We lose time too in the dragged-out execution of even necessary things. Sleeping, eating and the time taken to transition from one activity or location to another can be done with more accuracy and in less time.

Chapter 9

Interruptions

If it's not leading you towards your goals, it certainly is taking you away from them.

An interruption is a derailment from someone or something influencing you to abruptly spend quality time on or with it. They cause unnecessary breaks, stops or pauses in activity continuity thereby hampering concentration and reducing personal efficiency. Whether from people, gadgets or issues, interruptions are not productive since they hinder the continuity of an activity, impede the completion of important projects, and prevent the maximization of blossoming opportunities, potential, and purpose. Thus, interruptions rob us of the time dedicated to the completion of different - important activities.

Most interruptions or interrupters come promising to take just a minute or two and to give you something worthwhile in the end. The moment you give in to them, however, they cart away as much of your time as they possibly can, stalling your assignment and leaving you with little gain. They are killers of dreams, paralyzers of ideas and limiters of potential; they represent a danger to life and self-fulfilment.

In the book of Nehemiah, Sanballat, Tobiah, and Geshem, served as the perfect example of interrupters.

> *Now it came to pass, when Sanballat and Tobiah and Geshem the Arabian and the rest of our enemies heard that I had built the wall and that there was no breach left therein (though at that time I had not set up the doors upon the gates) that Sanballat and Geshem sent unto me saying, Come, let us meet together in some one of the villages in the plain of Ono. But they thought to do mischief. And I sent messengers unto them, saying, I am doing great work so that I cannot come down: why should the work cease, whilst I leave it and come down to you?*
>
> -   Nehemiah 6: 1 -3

From the scripture extract, it can be stated confidently that Sanballat, Tobiah and Geshem only came to distract Nehemiah, to interrupt and to make sure Nehemiah did not accomplish his goal – a prank or mere mischief targeted at his work programme. There are Sanballats, Tobiahs and Geshems waiting to meet you at every task just for fun. They show up when you are in the middle of something important and propose a pause. They come as people, other activities or unscheduled issues often demanding that you hold over important projects for later. In the end, you lose time and effectiveness.

Not all interruptions are out of mischief. Learn the difference and learn not to turn away those in genuine need of your attention. Nehemiah, perceptively said "No, you are not going to cause me to stop what I am doing because it is far more important than what you are trying to make me do. Go find someplace else or someone else to distract or interrupt." But his wave of the hand was not enough. The interrupting men kept on, just as most interruptions and interrupters do. More decisiveness is needed in combatting interruptions. While distractions steal time; interruptions are outside influences that interfere with the smooth running of activity and waste our time. More generally, we let ourselves be distracted by side attractions, while interruptions are mostly propagated by others. However, they lead to the same results – time, resource, and opportunity wastage.

Interruption Sources

1. The Mobile Phone

One of the greatest sources of distraction and interruption today is the mobile phone. We find people running to get their mobile phones whenever they receive even a beep. They abandon what they are doing, an interruption that can be rather too frequent.

Letting yourself get so remote-controlled by interruptions engenders time wastage. Streams of thought and even great ideas get lost in the process. It is a noted fact that bright ideas often occur spontaneously when a person is in the course of carrying out an activity. Losing focus from highly sensitive or important tasks to aimlessly skim through your phone is ill-advised. It disrupts the workflow, suspends the flow of thought processes and takes the work to a restart or initial position all over.

2. Visits/visitors

Having an unannounced stop by your home or office or during study hours is another form of interruption. Such guests often indicate that they will take just a few seconds of your time, but end up taking far too much of it. This practice is particularly common in schools and offices. A friend stops by and rattles about a bunch of issues just when the lecturer is about to give a life-changing principle, for example. Even a minute of interruption can be very costly.

It is great to be a good listener, someone to talk and share experiences with, but when this is associated with frequent interruptions, proceed with caution. In the same way, great as being cheerful and appreciative is pleasant, it is inconsiderate for everyone in your office or class to stop by for a chat every time. The completion of your assignment, the realization of your goals, and the fulfilment of your purpose depend on time; how you use it, and what you spend it on. As such, overly entertaining interruptions and time wasters can greatly affect your goal-realization process.

Dealing with Interruptions

1. Interruptions lead to a break in the smooth flow of focal activity.
2. They lead to the loss of important thought trains.
3. They interfere with task completion, goal realization and purpose fulfilment.
4. They waste time, break concentration, lead to loss of focus, and reduce overall performance and productivity.

Four ways of dealing with these interruptions are as follows:

1. **Learn to say 'No'**

By outrightly saying "No", most interruptions can be done away with without much harm. This, in a way, equally reinforces self-discipline. The defence that people need to be served or helped by your attention must be measured against the fact that you can't please everybody and that not everybody is worth pleasing. Lending a helping hand to others has to be evaluated against the implication that in the process you might neglect to complete your assignment. People will keep coming for as long as they get a listening and empathetic ear. And so you might need to choose between duty and external serviceability.

It hardly needs stressing that not every phone call needs to be answered immediately after the phone rings; not every conversation needs to be entertained instantly; not every activity has to be promptly welcomed. If a thing is not as important as what you are currently working on, it should wait and if the interruption or interrupter cannot wait, they are welcome to leave. You are to weigh the value of every interruption by its results. Defend the turf of your time and assignment from mischief makers. Stand up to interruptions and protect that which is precious and priceless – your time.

> *"And I sent messengers unto them, saying, I am doing great work so that I cannot come down: why should the work cease, whilst I leave it and come down to you?"*
> *(Nehemiah 6: 3)*

Just as you do not litter money, you should not litter time. A polite 'No' is often enough in this respect. We have different paths and assignments to fulfil, each unique and so trying to please others rather than carrying out our duty is detrimental to our destinies. For this reason, it can crisply be put that one has to cut any unhealthy company before it cuts off one's destiny.

2. Plan your day

A plan or schedule outlines the things to be done within a definite period. It may be sketched or printed. A well-planned day allocates time for activity beginning and completion, giving little room for time mismanagement, although ideally, it should make room for unforeseen happenings. When well followed, a schedule enhances control and concentration and focuses on the task to be executed at any given time. Also, popup activities can easily be identified and scheduled for a later time.

In your schedule, allocate quality time to more important activities and less time to not-so-important ones. Importance is given to activities that speed you towards fulfilling your life purpose. In this matrix, excepting emergencies and urgencies, phone calls can be answered at later, more convenient times. You can go through your emails or messages later, at a scheduled and more appropriate time. You can wisely anticipate the nature of notifications you are likely to receive from particular people to gauge their emergency. Some will never try to reach you at odd hours unless it's urgent. Failing to promptly attend to emergencies can be disastrous.

In this respect, you cannot have people stopping by or paying you visits at home or the office just anytime they feel bored or need relief. Don't let them steal your time. Refuse to be interrupted or distracted when studying or when focused on important tasks. Set clear rules about when you are available and when you are not. The more you value your time, the more others will give it value. Although we were created to be at the service of others, we must be ready to avoid going to battles that will end up having no spoils. We must value and guard our time jealously, making sure it is never at the mercy of wasters. If you allow people to interrupt you at will, you are, in effect, telling them that your time is not valuable.

3. Shun unhealthy environments

Being in an interruptive environment predicates interruptions. The way out is simply to shun such an environment. It is arduous and energy-depleting trying to maintain concentration in such a setup. And it doesn't have to be a continuously raucous situation as occasional breaks are all it takes to keep you destabilized and underproductive. You should take responsibility for the interruptions you cause or bear and get rid of them. This might not augur well with everyone around you, however, you must keep in mind that you alone know your destination and what it takes. Pursuit of that destination might entail stepping on some toes. It is costlier to be held back by what others say or do. So, get up and walk away.

Every visit, meeting, gathering or conversation has its duration. Staying on longer than necessary becomes wrong. Keep to the required duration and do not allow yourself to be talked into prolongation. Hold time to the highest of standards and be ready to give up what it takes to save it.

4. Discipline yourself

It takes discipline to get it right and to properly deal with unhealthy habits. If you can identify the times when you cause your interruptions, or when you procrastinate or get distracted, you can reclaim that time by simply disciplining yourself and those around you to refrain from such limiting habits. This entails giving up on one or more patterns or indulgences to get another. Although it seldom feels good while it is on, the future rewards are always worth it.

Key Points

1. What you spend time doing, and how you manage interruptions is a determinant factor in whether or not you realize your life goals.
2. Interruptions
   - prevent the completion of important assignments;
   - lead to the loss of thought train and important ideas;
   - breaks the smooth continuity of an activity;
   - wastes time, and disrupts concentration and focus;
   - greatly reduce overall performance and productivity.
3. You can neither help nor attend to everyone, so trying to please everyone is a doomed project: do your work, not that of others.
4. To efficiently deal with interruptions:
   - Learn to say 'No'
   - Plan your day
   - Shun unhealthy environments
   - Apply Self-discipline

Chapter 10

Sleep

Love not sleep, lest thou come to poverty; open thine eyes, and thou shalt be satisfied with bread.

- *Prov20: 13*

Highly recommended after, and even during, the work day, sufficient rest enables the brain to be properly prepped for more activity. The difficulty is drawing the line between laziness and adequate rest. Excessive rest is the harbinger of lacklustre performance and failure.

Calculate — If you sleep eight hours a day, by the time you are thirty years old, you would have slept off ten years. Worse, more sleep inclines us to even more, leading to a laidback underachieving lifestyle. Although it feels good rolling in bed, yawning and comfortably relaxed, unnecessarily long hours of sleep are bad investments. It is a collision course to mediocrity and poverty. Historically, important and ground-breaking strides and innovations are not associated with too much sleep but with taxed sleepless nights. Redolent inactivity is one of the causes of hard drugs that induce waste of life and time.

Success is a time-consuming journey, which argues for the need for judicious time use. In squandered time is squandered productivity. Anyone who loves his bed and sleeps beyond measure is not qualified for the journey of purposeful living.

Managing Rest

Too much sleep today, too much slumber tomorrow, robs tomorrow of grace. Too much comfort from your bed today, enough torment from poverty tomorrow. Open your eyes while it is day and you will be satisfied with bread. The physical consequences of excessive rest and sleep are not the worst from it. For there is the added feeling of passivity which snowballs into restive feelings of uselessness. In the end, the indolent tilts over to despair and generates a toxic atmosphere for others. It can be investigated as true that an attitude of hopelessness is both implosive and explosive; in either case, it is internally and externally devastatingly destructive.

How long wilt thou sleep, O sluggard? When wilt thou arise out of thy sleep? Yet a little sleep, a little slumber, a little folding of the hands to sleep: So shall thy poverty come as one that travelleth, and thy want as an armed man

-   Proverbs 6:9-11

Enough Sleep is a function of quality rather than just quantity. That is why sleeping for long does not guarantee that you will feel strong and refreshed when you wake. There are equally other factors to be considered. A line in the eBook *200 Secrets of Success* has it that we generally don't need more than six hours of sleep a day for a full recovery. If we literarily hang on to that statement, we can gain as much as 120 hours a month by cutting down our daily sleep time from ten to six hours. Applied to gainful ventures, 120 hours can be quite a haul of gains. Stretched to a twelve-month year, the time and gains become exponential. Since lying down is default inertia, it requires some effort to break the habit. Yet all that is needed is determination aided by the knowledge that excessive sleep is unnecessary and unproductive.

Quality Sleep

Sleeping just adequately is one other easy way to reclaim time for more productive pursuits. Remember that what you put in your time machine today will serve as the basis for your future results. Poverty, boredom, hopelessness and lack of fulfilment will most surely proceed from an exaggerated investment in sleep.

How the Body System Works

Just as women know of their menstrual cycle, we should all know our body metabolism and the best quality sleep time. Experts recommend going to bed before 10:00 p.m. although each person has unique moments when things seem to fall best into place. It is for each of us to identify optimal periods in our individual lives and make the most of them. A couple of factors have been proven to have effects on our sleep cycles. Prominent of these are:

1. Diet

The rule of thumb about feeding in respect of sleep is: do not eat to dullness. Excessive eating, especially at night before going to bed and during working hours, leads to heaviness that in turn requires more hours of sleep for vitality to be regained. Your diet should help to maximize your energy and mental clarity, rather than make you dizzy. It should be for strength and not for drunkenness. Nutritionists and health experts discourage any eating after 07:00 p.m. They further advise against eating close to bedtime and that not all foods are recommended to be eaten at any period of the day food.

Eating much is discouraged both during the day and at night. Also, a recommended food item does not give you the license to gluttony. Even healthy foods need a measured intake. For the most part, you only need enough of what can take care of your energy and health needs.

2. Your mood before bed

Going to bed happy helps keep you relaxed, giving you the liberated feel of quality rest even in a short sleep. It would appear the principle of inertia dominates even here so that a stirred good mood remains active even in sleep. By the same principle, a worried mind continues in restless inquietude even while in sleep, which does not help to rest the body. If possible, resolve all problems before going to bed. You may listen to soothing music or something inspirational to lull you to sleep, especially if you have difficulty falling asleep. Mental states influence rest. One reason why some people wake up from sleep feeling rather tired is that they carried worry to sleep. By this assumption, the happier and more relaxed one is, the less time will be needed for quality rest. Such a one wakes up rejuvenated and more vibrant.

On the same line of thought, it is recommended that we go to bed with expectations and plans for the day(s) ahead. When you go to bed with a plan, and an eagerness to embark on or continue work on a project, your subconscious prepares your biological clock for timely action. And if you are up while the world sleeps, you gain on time and undistracted concentration. Having something to wake up and do, cuts down on idle sprawling or oversleeping This argues for the need to plan. Without a concrete plan or program, the motivation to rise tends to be so low that it seems useless to even try – what's the point in waking up early if you will spend that time at nothing? And beyond morning plans, there should be worthwhile activity schedules for quality periods of each day. The closer such activities are focused on your core goals, the better.

This takes us once more to the necessity of prioritizing activities. It is recommended that you foreground activities which drive your passion, a project that has been unduly delayed, or one that is hard to start. That is where to invest time wrested from sleep and other activities for more productive and rewarding outcomes. Make sure then to plan on how to spend reclaimed time and this will motivate you to reclaim even more time from waste.

Key Points

1. Enough Sleep is a function of quality rather than just quantity.
2. Quality sleep can be attained in a shorter time through;
   - Knowing how your body system works
   - Avoiding excessive and close-to-bedtime eating
   - Going to bed in a good mood
3. Excessive sleep is a collision course to mediocrity and poverty.
4. Expectations will motivate your time of rising from bed; so plan on how to employ the time you gain.

Chapter 11

Transitioning

The time some people spend switching from one activity to another or moving from one location to another is often indicative of the extent of their respect for time. The trouble is they think they have time.

Self-Test

If you were late for a very important meeting, exam, job interview, or a rare opportunity, would you spend the same time in bathing, eating or commuting, as you do on a normal day? Of course, the answer is no, and for obvious reasons – the urgency of the appointment. This argues for a higher life pulse, informed by time consciousness. We should be time-conscious even when there is no need for urgency. The effect would be seen in the amount of week or month time gains we will make. Why keep forfeiting time to sluggish behaviour that robs you of time advantages?

Food for Thought

There are sidelines to this thought preference, but it is worth wondering whether it is worth your while to use up thirty to sixty minutes of your time trekking or spend a couple of hundred francs on the fare. Covering distances that would cost a few francs, some people trek even when it unwisely means using up much time. Trekking as a form of exercise is highly encouraged, but the context must be closely scrutinized. It just might be better to spend a few francs and save valuable time. Unlike money, time spent is not retrievable. If one has time, one can always invest it to make more money whereas no amount of money can buy time. When it comes to dealings involving time vis-à-vis other resources, we must be careful not to focus on immediate value or rewards only; the long-term and general importance of what we do needs to be considered also.

Time remains a fantastic currency with which you can carry out various activities for great rewards, resources, and money, but there is absolutely nothing you can do to get more time. For this reason, it is expedient that you be ruthless and wise in the way you manage or save time. It starts with saving only a few minutes deliberately and then cumulatively expanding the haul. It is suggested that you speed up mundane activities and transitions to speed up your life. Speed gives gusto and adds enthusiasm. At the same time, it makes more time available for priorities, which is preparedness for greater opportunities. It is better to be prepared for an opportunity and not have one than to have one and not be prepared for it. There always will be something better to do with saved time.

We may never have the time to do all the things we would like to do, but we have sufficient time to do the things that are important to us. Each day seems insufficient mostly because much is sacrificed to time wasters, sluggishness being among the often overlooked ones that silently, slowly and progressively eat up time.

Key Points

1. Unlike money, time spent is not retrievable. If one has time, one can always invest it to make more money whereas no amount of money can buy time

2. To save more time, be speedy and accurate.

3. We may never have the time to do all the things we would like to do, but we have sufficient time to do the things that are important to us

4. To manage time wisely, match what you stand to gain now with what you might lose in the future. Be wise

Part Four

Time Management Tips

It's never too late to change your life for the better. You don't have to take huge steps. Making even the smallest changes to your daily routine can make a big difference.

-   Alpha Wiser

So far we have analyzed and proposed ways of dealing with forms of distraction from the proper management of time, a rather negative approach. Pitfalls have been pointed out that should be avoided. The other perspective of time management, on the positive side, is the value of motivators or enhancers. Here is a catalogue of some useful ones to be made use of:

Chapter 12

Time Management Enhancers

If you're serious about changing your life, you'll find a way. If you're not, you'll find an excuse.

- Jen Sincero

1. A Routine

The secret of your future is hidden in your daily routine.

- Mike Murdock

John C. Maxwell, put it this way; *"you will never change your life until you change something you do daily. The secret to your success is found in your daily routine."* Have a routine and stick to it. Know what you will be doing on Monday, Tuesday and every day of the week. Know at what time you will be at them and stick to the schedule. It may not be comfortable and it need not be. It is enough that you judge the process to be important and be disciplined enough to follow through. Repeated over and over, routines become life habits.

Planning is the strong arm of efficiency and has the following positive elements:

- It gives you charge over your day.
- It gives you a definite sense of direction.
- It enhances concentration and focus, as it cuts down on irrelevance and zooms on necessity.
- It keeps you alert to derailments.
- It is a productivity enhancer.

2. Priority Consciousness

Effective planning is equally a correlative of prioritization, which happens to be the lifeline of efficient living. Any routine that doesn't focus on pursuits that matter to your life's mission and worthwhile interests will often yield minimal valuable results. The most efficient routine, which in turn translates to greater productivity, is that which is centered around your core life priorities. No rule requires that important activities be carried out first, but simply that the convenient and appropriate schedule be respected when it comes. Prioritizing easily differentiates important from non-important activities.

Attribution of appropriate, better, quality, more or less time to each follow suit.

Popular prioritization theories have placed activities into the following categories:

Important and Urgent: Tasks that need to be done right away.

Important, but not urgent: Important Tasks, but not tightly time-bound. You can decide when to do them, but not before the first category.

Urgent, but not important: Tasks that demand our attention immediately, warranting that we do them as soon as possible, but provide no lasting value when completed.

Not important and Not Urgent: These are usually leisure activities and distractions too – things we don't need to do but end up doing anyway because of the fleeting feeling of satisfaction they give.

The ABCDE method

Brian Tracy, in a bid to better explain the concept of prioritization and the correlation they have with rewards and consequences, categorized these activities as follows

A (Must do) activities: Important and Urgent.

Completing them comes with the greatest long-term and meaningful rewards, while not completing them can lead to severe consequences. They are to be handled first, or at an appropriate time. He advises that if you have more than one "A" task, you can further prioritize them as A-1, A-2, and so on.

B (Should do) activities: Important, but not urgent.

Mild rewards and consequences, not like A activities.

C (Can do) activities: Urgent, but not important.

Lesser in rewards and consequences – usually no consequences at all.

D activities: Activities that can be delegated.

E activities: Activities to be Eliminated.

Distractions fit right here: Least reward even when engaged in, and little or no consequences when shunned. You are better off eliminating them.

"The rule is that you should never do a B task when there is an A task left undone, or a C task when there are A and B tasks left undone." (Brian Tracy)

3. The Art of Delegation

You don't have to do everything by yourself. The secret to success in delegation is to find someone who can do, very well, the things you hate, don't necessarily have to do, or are not good at – someone who majors in your minors. It is about handing over certain tasks to experts in the concerned fields so you can pay more attention to your "A" level activities: the 20% of activities that make up for 80% of your life's results.

If you find that some other person can execute an activity better than you, or that you don't necessarily need to do it for the results to be excellent, delegate that activity and get on to something that invariantly needs your attention. Remember that although we cannot do everything, sufficient time has been given to us to do the most important things. Stick to your lane and trust delegable, and trivial tasks to competent parties. Reserve your time, energy, and resources for their most productive use.

4. Avoid Sloth

Sloth takes up large portions of time, and so must be avoided. From it we have no fruits to show, being barren in essence. It is an enemy, as is any activity that uses up your time unproductively. Worse, as the saying goes, an idle mind is the devil's workshop. The habit of diligent and efficient activity must be cultivated to take over from laziness and idleness which yield time wastage and unavoidable poverty. The habitation of the industrious is never without bread.

Slothfulness casteth into a deep sleep, and an idle soul shall suffer hunger.
Seest thou a man diligent in his business? He shall stand before kings; he shall not stand before mean men.

- *Proverbs 19:15, 22:29*

Sloth and an unplanned day accounts for a lack of effectiveness as people drag themselves through each activity, taking an unnecessary forever on assignments. This way, they delay the commencement of the next task by wasting time on the current one, a thing that can be avoided by a little programming and some speeding up with purposefulness.

5. Efficiency over Busyness

To be busy is to engage in work, while to be efficient is to engage in purposeful or goal-oriented work. It is possible to be busy without being efficient. The catch is what you are busy doing. To be efficient is to spend quality time, energy and resources on activities that are of great consequence, pursuits that are determinants in the accomplishment of life goals.

Efficiency takes you one step closer to completing your life assignment.

One of the ways we misuse time is by doing, very well, what should not be done in the first place. Working continuously for a whole day and having no rest is no proof of proper management of time. The relation of your activity to your life goals is what gives it value and efficiency. Being busy over trivialities; majoring in minors, is not effective time management. Spending more time than is necessary, on any activity, also accounts for poor time usage. It is via efficiency that effective time management gains value. There is therefore the need to practice efficiency over busyness!

Efficiency bonds with planning – documenting a vision of how you would want your day or future to look. You chart out a course of action so that nothing takes you by surprise and nothing irrelevant takes prominence. A plan well followed gives little room for distractions. It checks the unforeseen and potentially unproductive interactions or interruptions. This way, you take control of your day, wielding the power to engage or not engage in any activity. This will keep you from thoughtlessly or spontaneously jumping into the boats of others at their beck and call but choose wisely, according to the relevance of the activity to your programme.

Look at the following activity schedule for a given day:

- *Morning meditation and reflection*

- *Writing a book*
- *Going to school*
- *Personal study (reading a book)*
- *Taking a bath*
- *Eating*
- *Leisure and relaxation*

For efficiency or best time management results, allocate less time to less attention-needing activities like eating, bathing and leisure, which are routine, non-taxing processes. Meditation, writing and study should profit from the time gained because they are closer in context to your end goals. They are core life priorities, whose accomplishment directly impacts the direction, quality, and overall effect of your life. This evaluative alignment of activities enhances your accountability to yourself vis-à-vis your final goal, overall productivity and efficiency. Therefore, to be more efficient and productive, we must plan forward, and prioritize.

6. Activity compatibility

Certain activities can be executed simultaneously to gain extra time. Such activities may include listening to tapes along with sports walks or driving. Listening to gospel messages, music or motivational tapes for personal growth and empowerment, can be done with increased time allocation and gains if paired with jogging, gym workouts, driving or travelling. Also, news updates can be listened to during meals. We know what works best for us as individuals, however, the idea of pairing compatibles is a quick time-gain trick. Save time the best you can.

We should, however, be careful not to get into trouble by trying to yoke incompatibles – activities we find difficult to focus on at the same time and be at our optimal best, which then spell doom. It is best to stay focused on one activity than to jumble up incompatibles. Complete your chosen activity in time and in the best way possible before the next. Better be speedy than be confused.

In this respect, it is sometimes difficult to incorporate leisure into our day because negative overtones about it frame it as a distraction. Being a source of relaxation, leisure is good as it gives the mind, body, spirit, nerves and brain a chance to rest. Being planned and executed for a particular purpose positively reinforces the best in the person. Purposeful leisure is different from compromise which has to be opposed by principled behaviour even when it hurts. The good news is that tough and principled people are so often preferred to soft dilly-dallying ones. If you have anything to offer, then you need to be tough and principled enough to defend it. Holding your time, standards and principles in high regard is an indication of a growth-conscious and goal-centered mind.

7. Diligence

Diligence confronts the idea of a goal being boring, which is often a prejudicial perceptual fault based on ignorance. A perceived goal may be difficult but engagement enthusiasm dissolves the difficulty. The temptation against diligence often also results from a lacklustre attitude rather than from the activity itself. Succumbing to boredom blossoms into procrastination on urgent matters. And so we don't have many options outside diligent application to duty. Pushing forward activity to an already cumbersome 'tomorrow' is no way of getting it done. And so, it is wiser to find the enthusiasm within us to face our tasks despite our emotional inclinations.

8. Proactivity and Promptness

Today presents us with the opportunity to do something worthwhile with our lives, but it is often overtaken by the tomorrow syndrome. Tomorrow always seems ideal for work or its completion, the ideal time to do everything. It is seen as better than stretching a little beyond our comfort zones or going the extra mile today. The punctual assertion: "I will do that tomorrow", invites the individual to heap up work for another day, the congested infinity of tomorrow. The rule of thumb seems to be to keep nothing for tomorrow that should be done today.

Tomorrow answers all lazy excuses for activities that could be carried out today to completion. When we push to tomorrow and overload it with even greater workloads, the said 'tomorrow' becomes inevitably boring and overwhelming. At the risk of being a jumbled doggerel, let it be said that today is the tomorrow of yesterday and what you carried forward from yesterday has no guarantee of being done tomorrow. Between the successful person and the wishful thinker lies doing today and pushing off to tomorrow.

How we procrastinate

Anytime I promise to do something "tomorrow", I know, somehow, that I am procrastinating. And whenever my choices of activities for that day are thoroughly scrutinized, I am usually found wanting nine out of ten times. Sufficient time was made available for the activity I planned on pushing forward to be adequately completed that day and on time. This time was simply at the mercy of unproductive pleasantries.

Perhaps the mother of all false assumptions is the assertion that we have to feel like doing something before doing it. It has to be banished. In as much as motivation is a starter and booster of tasks, a disciplined person must take up duty, irrespective of personal convenience. The successful person carries out today what the wishful thinker is thinking of doing someday to come.

9. Clarity

A major cause of stagnation often brought on by a lack of clarity as to the true nature of the task at hand, insufficient knowledge or a disorganized mind or plan, emotion or environment, is indecision. One way around indecision is to develop clarity – a succinct and lucid knowledge of what is important, the plan to be followed, and the consequences of carrying or not carrying it out. If the necessary facts are understood and an organized scale of preference mapped out, decision-making, and consequently efficient time usage, becomes quite easy.

The worst-case scenario is simply to start doing something from any point. Yet even this is preferred to doing nothing at all, for there are lessons to be learned in the process and a serendipitous find might just straighten the path to success. That is why it is to be preferred to indecision which keeps us at a standstill. It is decisiveness that gives value to the saved time from time wasters. Simply abstaining from time waste is no proof of efficient time management. Thus, if you avoided movie watching, video games or other pastimes for the whole day – if before then you got up at the crack of dawn or switched off your phone from distractions or even volunteered to be kept under house arrest, these would amount to very little if you do not apply the gained time to a worthwhile goal, to something that matters.

Key Points

To manage your time effectively,
- Stick to a routine
- Avoid sloth
- Be efficient rather than busy
- Plan your day
- Prioritize
- Pair up compatibles and vice versa
- Be diligent, shunning the tomorrow syndrome
- Do the necessary, not what you feel.

Chapter 13

Time Management Motivators

1. Knowledge of Purpose

Purpose is the intent or reason for living, your ordained mission or divine assignment. It is the 'why you were created' that gives meaning to 'what you have at your disposal'. Knowledge of your mission and your application to it should keep you focused and distraction-free. It is knowledge of God's intentions for your life, and what he requires of you. It helps you to identify what type of activities to prioritize, when and how to start, and how to make it to that expected end. Knowing your purpose and knowing what you need to fulfil it gives you the urge to start your journey and thriftily keep it to the end. Like driving on the highway, the journey towards fulfilling purpose is fraught with dangers; distractions are fatal.

2. Having a Life Vision

Vision is the reason for a life of direction and focus, the source of commitment and the fuel for tenacity. It is the ability to see into the ordained future, a mental picture of your expected end about your purpose and present position, and a glimpse of your ideal self. *"Where there is no vision, the people perish..." (Proverbs 29:18).*

Elsewhere the bible reads:

> *I will stand upon my watch, and set me upon the tower, and will watch to see what he will say unto me, and what I shall answer when I am reproved. And the LORD answered me, and said, Write the vision, and make it plain upon tables, that he may run that readeth it. For the vision is yet for an appointed time, but at the end, it shall speak, and not lie: though it tarries, wait for it; because it will surely come, it will not tarry.* (Habakkuk 2:1-3)

There can be no purposeful and meaningful "running", without clarity of vision. Having a picture of what God intends for your life will stir up a desire to get there as soon as possible rather than wasting time in a run in the wrong direction. With this high sense of expectation and direction comes the inevitable need for proper time and resource management to foster self-discipline and better concentration.

3. Goals

Set goals you would hope to achieve and with these goals, affix specific times to realize them. Goal setting highly motivates time management, providing awareness of all you are expected to do and the habits or sacrifices to be made to realize a predetermined goal. Setting goals enhances focus and concentration, and eliminates distractions. They keep you always on the right path to God-ordained dreams, jealously placed in you for God's glory and your happiness. Detailed goals make for focused and intentional living.

One way towards efficiency in time and life management is effective goal setting. Effective goals are goals that centre around your core values, purpose or life mission. If they do not affect the pace of your core values or mission, then your goals do not relate to the progress of your life assignment. In that case, is a sure path to wasted efforts and sadness. Effective goals are the trunk on which the tree of your activities grows; their accomplishments are vital to your being, fulfilment, happiness and success.

It is important to note here that a change in routine is one major factor that qualifies intentionality in your quest for a better life. If your routine, after you claim to have set goals, remains the same as it was before you set these goals, I think it will be safe to say that you are not serious about your claims for a better life and that nothing will change in your results. The essence of setting goals is to make for clarity of direction and action. A change in routine is one defining proof that you are serious about your goals. Therefore, if nothing changes in your routine, nothing about your results will change, no matter how many times you write down your goals.

4. Action Plans

Detailing of the goal, along with timing constitutes an action plan. These facilitate the execution of goals on a daily, weekly or monthly basis. They are the way to optimal use of your time because they take away wasteful idleness and are a monitoring and assessing instrument for time-bound progress. They should, of course, engender prioritized goals. It is said that he who fails to plan has in effect planned to fail. Planning implies focus and greater effectiveness.

5. Principles

Principles inspire decision-making and are the guidelines you live by, somewhat like action regulators that generate moral stamina against the drawbacks of your life. Like other motivators, being principled keeps you focused and protective of your time. Principles engender integrity which becomes a moral compass of actions, character, behaviour and responsibility. Principles decide what you do or do not tolerate. They are your standards against compromising activities or tendencies. When principles and standards guide actions, time wasters are dismissed.

6. Visualization

Picturing yourself successful, working in your chosen field and living the life of your dreams boosts the realization of these desires. They are like the foretaste of the glory. They set your mind to work in collaboration with all the forces of nature towards the realization of your mental picture. Visualization differs from daydreaming in that it is better structured and is closely fastened to scheduled activities. It sets the subconscious to work, judiciously and rightly dividing your time into pursuits that will take you closer to crystalizing the object of your imagination.

7. Decisive Action

Motivators, beyond being mentally convincing, should spring you into action that is anchored to your goals with a great sense of direction. They are imagination sticklers from which come great ideas and action boosters. When anchored to efficient time management and promptness, imagination stirs us to unstoppable progress and accomplishments. The consolation is that all your dreams can come true if you efficiently manage your resources and channel them towards your dream goals. 'Well done' is further up the ladder than 'well said' or 'well heard'. We are called upon to take action and not just stir up great dreams. The devastating 'had I known' statement is a function of daydreaming rather than visualizing unto action.

That said, there are nonetheless some things you just should not have time for, some battles you shouldn't waste time on, and some conversations, gatherings and confrontations you shouldn't be part of. Understand that you don't have any extra time, that each passing moment, takes you to your latter days. Take an inventory of your life and stop wasting time on things that have no relation to your purpose.

Key Points

Time management motivators are the positive contraries of time wasters and enjoin you to:
- Know our purpose
- Have a vision
- Set goals
- Draw actions plans
- Be principled
- Visualization
- Decisiveness and promptness in action

Chapter 14

What to Spend Time on

1. Building Capacity

Relevance is a function of worth or value – what you have to offer, and value only increases via a conscious application to consistently build relevant capacity. Therefore, those who actively engage in building capacity – going the extra mile to learn and grow will never fail to be in demand.

Spend time investing, and building up spiritual, intellectual and physical capacity. Meditation on the word of God is one way to build up your faith. In this respect, the Bible is probably the most important book you can read. Grow in knowledge and skill by reading good and relevant books or literature, attending seminars and going on research trips. Study to qualify for the blossoming opportunities that will surely come your way. Remember that opportunity only favours the prepared – those with in-demand value to offer. For physical health, exercise frequently and adopt a proper diet. Refine your gifts, skills, abilities and talents to ready them for deployment.

Being informed and grounded has a way of improving self-esteem and respect. The time you are wasting could be channelled to such pursuits, building your intellectual, spiritual and physical abilities. Those who diligently invest time in these never fail to reap the rewards at the appropriate season. There is ample room at the top for those who work themselves up there through capacity building. No day then should pass by without you spending quality time building these pillars to ensure the lasting structure of your life and future. Read a book a day if you must, just don't waste time on unproductive pleasantries. They are worth your time, so give it to them. I mean, what else could be more important than investing quality time and resources to ensure that your future turns out as bright and beautiful as you have always wanted it to be?

2. Building, Refining and Maximizing Potential

After identifying your core – of or relating to purpose, passion, or interests – gifts, talents, or skills you will like to master, there is a need for you to get to the incubation stage of life. Separate yourself from the crowd and spend quality time building and refining these potentials till they grow, mature, ripen and are ready for deployment. The butterfly is proof that the caterpillar has gone through the process of incubation. No incubation, no breaking forth to glory. In like manner, your gifts, talents, skills and abilities (the wealth of your potential), to be fully developed, refined, and polished for deployment, need close attention. Identify and work on them till they become marketable. Opportunity only favours the prepared.

Everything Gets Better with Practice.

Some people look down on their inborn talents and waste time ogling at those of others. Their gifts sink and rot unappreciated by them. Working to build for yourself the skills and abilities you admire in others is a great thing to do; but completely neglecting your core talents and abilities in the process, is absurd. God made you unique for a reason. Your core will always be the springboard to true success. Outside the maximization and deployment of your in-built talents, you only get pseudo-success. We must accept and work with our talents as often as we can.

The size of the tree is never justified by the size of the seed because even a very small seed carries the life of its tree. The same goes for your potential and interests. No matter how small, apparently foolish or insignificant they may be, they carry the core of your success. It is foolishness to look down, ignore or throw them away, covetously desiring what belongs to another. Others too only had the seed they groomed, but accepted, worked with and refined them for deployment. Therefore, "what is" is not as important as "what it can become" or "what will be" if well catered for.

Quality Time Is the Keyword

To further pursue the seed-tree image, little attention is paid to the seed or even tree, however big or small it may be. But when the fruits get ripe, the tree becomes an instant attraction. Not many people care about intrinsic value. Until it is identified, refined, and tangibly deployed, they couldn't care less. Accept and work with what seeds you have been given and your fruits will make a way for you. Spend quality time on planting, nursing, nurturing, maturing, refining, polishing and getting them ready for deployment. That is the only way to true success. With sufficient practice and refinement, there is no telling how far your potential can take you.

"what is" is not as important as "what it can become"

---

3. Investing in your Passions, Ideas, and Creative Abilities

Every path, idea, ability, or passion can be monetized. Do the things you love, and have fun doing them, adding to it a means of getting paid for that pursuit. Your justification, inter alia, is that you only get to live once and that denying yourself the joy, satisfaction and fulfilment you get by living your dreams and exploring the full length of your creative abilities leaves you with little else to cherish life for. Spend time on your passions, exploring your creative abilities. In the process, it is expected that you will face challenges, fall or have some nasty turns. When you fall, get up, learn your lessons, and then try again; it is better to try and fail than fail to try for fear of failure. Happy, and fulfilled people spend their time doing the things they love. The rest pay them to do more. They seek fulfilment, and money follows. Without in any way contradicting the discourse in the previous chapter that you do not need to like what you must do before doing it, it is clear that doing what you love is the first step to a happy life.

4. Building Quality Relationships

Short and fragile, life is hardly worth living without family, and friends. Today you are young and vibrant; tomorrow one of your grandchildren will be reading your biography at your burial. It is not worth wasting your time now quarrelling with family rather than cherishing the moments with them.

Harriet Beecher Stowe said: "The bitterest tears shed on graves are for words left unsaid and actions left undone." And indeed we should not let this be our lot by playing the unforgiving child or parent now only to wail in the future for all the times we failed to be together because of trivial misunderstandings. Make the most of the time now; spend it with your loved ones.

The statement may be questioned by some critics, but no alternative to the homeliness of home has been found and there is no bond stronger than family love. Family is not just an important thing, but the best thing that can happen to anyone. Orphans and abandoned children would tell you how much they would give up just for an opportunity to stay under the same roof with those you call nagging mothers, stern fathers or disagreeable siblings.

5. Helping others and Making Valuable Contributions to the World

Our gifts are for giving and there is hardly a greater good than the zeal to genuinely help others. It is both fulfilling and rewarding as opposed to selfishness and complacent self-sufficiency which only leads to loneliness and frustration. It never pays to be selfish, not thinking about the welfare of others. Step out of your closet from time to time and make an effort to attend to the needy. Shelter the weak, give to the poor, the unable and those who in any way – financially, materially, or otherwise – are helpless or even temporally disadvantaged. In this, there is a great reward.

Use your gifts for the glory of God, impacting the lives of those you were created to impact by deploying your gifts and potential. Services and charity fall in this category of gifts to be given to others. Be the light around you to set others free from all forms of darkness: live for a purpose bigger than yourself. like trees that never eat their fruits or rivers that never drink their water and like the sun that shines out for others, you too should live for others and desire to be a blessing to your generation. It is worth spending time this way for the glory of God and the welfare of others. What you make available for others, God will make available for you.

6. Getting to Know and Serve God

Without God in the picture, forget it. All we have learnt and will ever learn or apply amounts to nothing. The old Catholic Catechism rattled our purpose of existence as follows: *God made us to love Him, to serve and to be happy with Him forever in heaven.* The simplicity of the statement could not be bettered, but at the end of the day, it seems all we are about here stands or falls on that simple claim. It is St Paul who says that if we live, we live for God and if we die, we die for God. Make it your aim to live for God, and to use all he has given, and will continually give you, to his glory.

Living Versus Existing

We get to live once; once to do the things we were created for and would love to do; this once to fulfil the divine purpose and run the lane of God's master plan for our lives; this once to spend time with family and loved ones; this once to love and know what it feels like to be loved; this once to lend a helping hand and to do good to those in need; this once to impact and change the lives of those we were ordained to change; this once to leave a legacy upon this earth; to be known for something. We have one chance only to stand out and charge out to fulfilment, realizing the things that give our lives meaning. We must therefore cherish our uniqueness, value our gifts, work on our strengths and build, refine and polish what skills we have, making sure to enjoy life to our later days.

This is a clarion call for us to live fruitfully and positively rather than merely exist; to be the best we can, not someone else's version of perfect; to be ourselves, act ourselves and appreciate whom we are created to be. In that life finally takes on its true purpose and meaning for us. The noted detail that no even number ever occupies the first place warns us to stop standing in the second position, behind others. We have the task to discover where we stand by divine placement: there is a first position for us all at our respective callings.

Key Points

Time already used cannot be reclaimed so making the most of it, and spending it the right way once at our disposal is wise:

1. Spend time investing in yourself building your spiritual, mental, intellectual and physical capabilities.
2. Spend quality time building, refining and maximizing your potential.
3. Follow your passions and creative abilities;
4. Spend time with family, loved ones and value-adding friends.
5. Spend time helping others.
6. Spend time using your gifts to the glory of God, impacting the lives of those you were created to impact as you deploy these gifts and potentials.
7. Spend time knowing and serving God.

Conclusion

The Choice is Yours

We, as individuals, are entirely responsible for our time and answerable for how we use it. If then we are to answer for it, we must take total control and decide how it is used. Like Muhammad Ali, you can invest your time today – working, in to become a champion tomorrow; you can also choose to waste your present time and struggle in the future. Choose wisely. Time, like life, follows the inflexible law of Cause and Effect; we shall reap just what we sow.

Sowing the right seeds into our time farms today guarantees abundant harvests tomorrow. How and on what we spend our time today decides what or who we become tomorrow. It is in this over-emphasized statement that the whole structure hangs or falls: Time management is life management; it can be likened to the ground in which seeds of the future are sown. The investments you make with your time today are for your future. Refining your gifts, skills, talents and abilities is building up your capacity and readying yourself for deployment will largely be to your benefit.

It is not a race of speed but of authentic consistency nursed in the diligent honing of inbuilt talents. It is the application of a gentle but incoercible persistence in refining the self to the best for service. It implies giving up on passing goals to reach permanent achievements. Windows operating system and Microsoft founder, Bill Gates, ranked the world's richest man by Forbes Magazine spent an average of 10 to 16 hours a day for some five years trying to develop computer programs. He attests that between the ages of 20 and 30, he did not once take one day off duty. He worked his life out, investing quality time in developing his gift, passion and talents, and not giving up when things turned tough. He held hard to his dream, vision and purpose of coming up with a revolutionary idea. It paid off and will pay off for anyone who borrows from his diligence.

Effective and efficient time management is the medium for success, fulfilment, happiness and affluence in the future, and it is a path that has no shortcuts. Chesterfield is echoed by

King David: "Teach us to number our days so that we may apply our hearts to wisdom" (Ps 90:12). Benjamin Franklin considered time to be "…the stuff life is made up of." We are to value it properly. And the time to start is now: for "If you would want to have tomorrow the things others won't have", Less Brown says, "…you must be ready to do today the things they won't do". One of the things they won't do is better manage their time, channelling it to conceived and productive goals.

"Know the true value of time; snatch it, seize it and enjoy every moment of it. No idleness, no laziness, no procrastination. Never put off until tomorrow what you can do today."

- *Lord Chesterfield*

To make a difference, you must be different, or better yet, act differently. Be about your business; every other thing is secondary.

I leave the reader to ponder on the following essential time and resource management narrative by Benjamin Franklin – an excerpt, for advice, rightly applied can transform:

"I stopt my Horse lately where

a great Number of People were collected at a Vendue of Merchant Goods. The Hour of Sale not being come, they were conversing on the Badness of the Times, and one of the Company call'd to a plain clean old Man, with white Locks, Pray, Father Abraham, what think you of the Times? Won't these heavy Taxes quite ruin the Country? How shall we be ever able to pay them? What would you advise us to? —Father Abraham stood up, and reply'd, "If you'd have my Advice, I'll give it you in short, for a Word to the Wise is enough, and many Words won't fill a Bushel, as Poor Richard says". They join'd in desiring him to speak his Mind, and gathering round him, he proceeded as follows:

"Friends," says he, "and Neighbours, the Taxes are indeed very heavy, and if those laid on by the Government were the only Ones we had to pay, we might more easily discharge them; but we have many others, and much more grievous to some of us. We are taxed twice as much by our Idleness, three times as much by our Pride, and four times as much by our Folly, and from these Taxes the Commissioners cannot ease or deliver us by allowing an Abatement. However, let us hearken to good Advice, and something may be done for us: 'God helps them that help themselves,' as Poor Richard says, in his Almanack of 1733.

"It would be thought a hard Government that should tax its People one-tenth Part of their Time, to be employed in its Service. But Idleness taxes many of us much more, if we reckon all that is spent in absolute Sloth, or doing of nothing, with that which is spent in idle Employments or Amusements, that amount to nothing. Sloth, by bringing on Diseases, absolutely shortens Life. Sloth, like Rust, consumes faster than Labour wears, while 'the used Key is always bright,' as Poor Richard says. 'But dost thou love Life, then do not squander Time, for that's the Stuff Life is made of,' as Poor Richard says.

How much more than is necessary do we spend in Sleep! Forgetting that 'The sleeping Fox catches no Poultry,' and that 'there will be sleeping enough in the Grave,' as Poor Richard says. If Time be of all Things the most precious, 'wasting Time' must be, as Poor Richard says, 'the greatest Prodigality,' since, as he elsewhere tells us, 'Lost Time is never found again; and what we call Time-enough, always proves little enough'. Let us then be up and be doing, and doing to the Purpose; so by Diligence shall we do more with less Perplexity. 'Sloth makes all Things difficult, but Industry all easy,' as Poor Richard says; and 'He that riseth late, must trot all Day, and shall scarce overtake his Business at Night.' While 'Laziness travels so slowly, that Poverty soon overtakes him,' as we read in Poor Richard, who adds, 'Drive thy Business, let not that drive thee,' and 'Early to Bed, and early to rise, makes a Man healthy, wealthy and wise.'

"So what signifies wishing and hoping for better Times. We may make these Times better if we bestir ourselves. 'Industry need not wish,' as Poor Richard says, and 'He that lives upon Hope will die fasting. There are no Gains, without Pains; then

Help Hands, for I have no Lands, or if I have, they are smartly taxed. And, as Poor Richard likewise observes, 'He that hath a Trade hath an Estate, and He that hath a Calling hath an Office of Profit and Honour.' But then the Trade must be worked at, and the Calling well followed, or neither the Estate nor the Office will enable us to pay our Taxes. — If we are industrious we shall never starve; for, as Poor Richard says, 'At the working Man's House, Hunger looks in, but dares not enter. Nor will the Bailiff nor the Constable enter, for Industry pays Debts, while Despair increaseth them,' says Poor Richard. — What? Though you have found no Treasure, nor has any rich Relation left you a Legacy, 'Diligence is the Mother of Good luck,' as Poor Richard says, and God gives all Things to Industry. Then 'plough deep, while Sluggards sleep and you shall have Corn to sell and to keep,' says Poor Dick. Work while it is called Today, for you know not how much you may be hindered To-morrow, which makes Poor Richard say, 'One Today is worth two Tomorrows,' and farther, 'Have you somewhat to do Tomorrow, do it To-day.

If you were a Servant, would you not be ashamed that a good Master should catch you idle? Are you then your own Master, be ashamed to catch yourself idle,' as Poor Dick says. When there is so much to be done for yourself, your Family, your Country and your gracious King, be up by Peep of Day. Let not the Sun look down and say, 'Inglorious here he lies.' Handle your Tools without Mittens; remember that 'the Cat in Gloves catches no Mice,' as Poor Richard says. 'Tis true there is much to be done, and perhaps you are weak handed, but stick to it steadily, and you will see great Effects, for 'constant Dropping wears away Stones, and by Diligence and Patience the Mouse ate in two the Cable; and little Strokes fell great Oaks,' as Poor Richard says in his Almanack, the year I cannot just now remember.

"Methinks I hear some of you say, 'Must a Man afford himself no Leisure?' — I will tell thee, my Friend, what Poor Richard says: 'Employ thy Time well if thou meanest to gain Leisure; and, since thou art not sure of a Minute, throw not away an Hour. Leisure is Time for doing something useful; this Leisure the diligent Man will obtain, but the lazy Man never,' so that, as Poor Richard says, 'a Life of Leisure and a Life of Laziness are two Things. Do you imagine that Sloth will afford you more Comfort than Labour?' No, for as Poor Richard says, 'Trouble springs from Idleness, and grievous Toil from need-less Ease. Many without Labour would live by their Wits only, but they break for want of Stock. Whereas Industry gives Comfort, and Plenty, and Respect; Fly Pleasures and they'll follow you. The diligent Spinner has a large Shift; and now I have a Sheep and a Cow, every Body bids me Good morrow,' all which is well said by Poor Richard.

...

I am,
as ever,
Thine to serve thee,
RICHARD SAUNDERS July 7, 1757

www.ingramcontent.com/pod-product-compliance
Lightning Source LLC
Chambersburg PA
CBHW050344160726
48002CB00001B/451